Summer in Connecticut

A POSITIVELY CONNECTICUT™ BOOK

Diane Smith

The Globe Pequot Press

GUILFORD, CONNECTICUT

Text design by LeAnna Weller Smith and Nancy Freeborn

Library of Congress Cataloging-in-Publication Data
Smith, Diane.
    Summer in Connecticut : a Positively Connecticut book / Diane Smith.—1st ed.
      p. cm.
    ISBN 0-7627-3051-X
      1. Connecticut—Description and travel. 2. Summer—Connecticut. 3. Connecticut—Social life and customs. 4. Connecticut—History, Local. I. Title.

F101.S55 2004
974.6'044—dc22
                                                                    2004044003

Manufactured in the United States of America
First Edition/First Printing

Contents

Fresh Flavors

Is there anything more mouthwatering than the fresh flavors that Connecticut's earth and sea yield in the heart of summer? Think of the sweetness of lobster, caught just hours earlier in the cold waters of Long Island Sound; the oysters and clams dredged from beds that once nourished the Native Americans who knew this land before the rest of us did. The only tastes that might compare are the foods we eat hot off the grill—the hamburgers invented in New Haven at Louis' Lunch, or perhaps the hot dogs that made Connecticut famous, dressed and prepared in our own unique style and carefully made according to old family recipes of the Germans and other wurst-loving immigrants who moved here. Each of these summer specialties ought to be accompanied by an ear of sweet corn, picked that very day by farmers in fields so close by, a fresh ear of corn or a juicy scarlet tomato may still be warm from the summer sun when you get it to the kitchen of your suburban home or city town house. Roadside farm stands remain abundant, even while our precious farmland is shrinking and threatened by development. Farmers' markets mushroom everywhere in summer, whether it's a few trucks tucked beneath an overpass just off Route 8, an urban "farm" in the center of New Britain sprouting exotic greens and herbs, or a field full of white tents on Ashlawn Farm in Lyme. The old dairy farm is now a scenic farmers' market where shoppers and vendors are surrounded by red barns, cows, and stone walls and the offerings include Connecticut-grown produce, seafood and meat, flowers, freshly baked pastries, and gourmet coffee beans, roasted in the old milk room.

Tired of the same old dishes you prepare every day? How about a food festival to enliven your taste buds? There's one for nearly every cuisine on the globe sometime this summer, and some combine a taste of each, a tease that will take you to new restaurants throughout the rest of the year.

The way to enhance these fresh flavors is by eating alfresco, whether out of the basket of berries you just picked at a local farm, on a balcony overlooking the city, in a restaurant courtyard with a jazz combo swinging softly as you dine, or on a rooftop as the sun sets and the stars come out. There are backyard barbecues, picnics in leafy parks, a shore dinner devoured while perched on sawed-off tree stumps at The Place, a clambake in a sandpit on the beach, or even a fresh-caught fish grilled on the deck of your boat. The season for fresh flavors in Connecticut is short, but oh so sweet!

The Sweet Life

Plink plink plink—the sound of ripe blueberries falling into a plastic bucket. On a warm July morning, Roy and Doris Newell are picking blueberries at Rose's Berry Farm in South Glastonbury. "With a little ingenuity there's a lot of ways you can use them," Roy says with a smile. "They're all delicious."

George Schmaltz has been coming here to pick berries for twenty years. Today he is filling a twelve-pound bucket. "Well, we'll freeze some of them, eat most, we'll make some into pies, and my grandchildren are waiting for some of them, too," he says as he bends to continue picking.

The farm is just a little over ten miles from downtown Hartford, but it feels like it's in the middle of Maine, with rolling green hills framing fields

of ripening blueberries and ruby-red raspberries. A woman is carefully picking the best of the latter. "That's a beauty," she says. How can she tell when a raspberry is ripe? Her answer is poetic: "When it feels like a cat's paw."

Sandi Rose and her husband, Henry, own the farm where they raise twenty varieties of blueberries, ranging from the quarter-sized Patriots to the dusky blue Collins variety. "A lot of people are no longer in a country situation," Sandi says. "So they just want to come out to the country and have a little picnic and do a little picking and do something fun with their family." The season begins with strawberry picking in June and continues with raspberries (June into October) and, later, blueberries (July to September). Later on apples, pumpkins, and even Christmas trees are offered.

The farm has been in the Rose family since 1910, selling fruit to farm stands all over the state. But every year some fifty thousand people trek to the farm to pick their own. Naturally Sandi is high on the nutritional values of the fresh berries. "The longer the blueberry is off the bush, the more you lose nutrients. That's another reason why people pick their own. Because if it's any fresher, it's still growing."

If all this is making you hungry, you're in luck. Every Sunday morning you can visit the farm not only to pick your own fruit but also to enjoy a hearty breakfast of pancakes or waffles, all topped with fresh berries, while you sit on a deck overlooking the fields. Customers delight in Sandi's berry jams, toppings, fruity vinegars, and farm-made pies.

Sandi loves farming: "You get to see a finished product." But, she notes, "you have this adversary—it's called the weather. We are the biggest gamblers around. We don't have to go to Foxwoods Casino. We gamble every day." During growing season running the farm is a round-the-clock job. Is Sandi ever tempted to say to her husband, Henry, "This is just too hard; let's do something else"?

"This time of year, about once a week!" she says with a laugh. So what keeps them going year after year? "Well," Sandi muses, "farming is not a job as much as it's a lifestyle."

On a warm summer's day, it's a lifestyle that's pretty sweet.

Strawberry Shortcake and Cream

For many of us summer doesn't really begin until we pop that first ripe sun-warmed strawberry into our mouths. Strawberry festivals are an annual tradition throughout Connecticut from Memorial Day through early June, and Rowayton—at the mouth of the Five Mile River—is no exception.

Here the strawberry tradition dates back to the days when this was an oystering community. That was when Rowayton United Methodist Church began dishing up its famous strawberry shortcake every Memorial Day weekend as a fund-raiser. The project continues, and it's a massive one.

Brandi Hayden, the director of music for the church, has taken over baking duties, and she loves it. "I only know how to bake in quantity. My mom and dad worked two jobs each, so even though there

were only four in my family, my mother only had time to cook on weekends, so she cooked everything in bulk. So baking five hundred servings of shortcake didn't seem so bad."

Brandi's shortcake is delicious, classic short-cake, not overly sweet, firm and biscuitlike, able to stand up to the juicy red berries. Each member of the church takes home a basket of strawberries to slice the night before, and then throughout the Memorial Day parade volunteers stir sugar into enormous bowls of sliced berries and whip up real whipped cream—thirty-six quarts of it! Still other volunteers run the cooled berries, cream, and shortcake across the street from the church to Pinkney Park, where Rowayton residents line up for their sweet old-fashioned treat.

The Best of
the Wurst

Is Connecticut the Hot Dog State?

Jane and Michael Stern, the road-food experts who search out the most memorable local eateries on the back roads of America, are convinced that it is. "Every part of America has different kinds of hot dogs. Even in Connecticut, from place to place they're prepared so differently, they're dressed so differently, and they're bunned so differently," Michael observes on that classic summertime treat.

What makes a hot dog great? Jane has some standards. "Hot dogs have had a very bad reputation because they're a kind of mystery meat tubes; you don't really know what you're eating, and the most someone will grudgingly tell you is it's beef or pork, but beef or pork what?" she muses. "The places that Michael and I adore in Connecticut really are careful about what goes into the hot dog. What the casing is made of, for instance—if it's natural or artificial. It makes a difference if it's grilled, if it's fried. It's like any food—you can make a mishmosh out of it or you can make it almost a gourmet experience."

One of their favorites is **Super Duper Weenie** in Fairfield. Observing the menu of New Englanders, Chicagoans, Dixie Dogs, Mighty Ities, and more, Jane says, "It's like a little map of the hot dog world that you can travel around. And they are snappy, snappy dogs."

Michael agrees. "Everything about Super Duper Weenie really is super duper. The hot dogs are special, the buns are from a real bakery, and the condiments—I mean, these are actually made-from-scratch condiments."

Owner Gary Zemola is a former chef at a fine restaurant in the SoNo section of Norwalk, and he emphasizes fresh ingredients. "We take actual fresh cucumbers, we peel them, we seed them, we grind them, salt them, get out the liquid, we pickle them and make our own relish right here." His dogs are made in Stratford by a family of German immigrants.

Gary knew what he wanted when he opened Super Duper Weenie. "The whole idea of this place was to taste a hot dog that was probably the way it was prepared maybe fifty or sixty years ago. They didn't have something that would have a shelf life of six months to a year. I wanted it to taste like something from a bygone era."

In a bygone era, **Rawley's**—another Fairfield classic—was someone's house. The front porch is now where you order dogs that are deep-fried, then grilled. Michael Stern calls Rawley's "the grand old man of southern Connecticut hot dog places. I don't know if they originated it, but they are really the upholders of the deep-fried technique."

Nick Frattaroli is Rawley's fourth owner since the eatery opened in the 1940s. "It's a tradition that's been carried on for years and years and years. We just kept it the same. We're not changing anything."

Jane sums up a Rawley's Special: "This would not win a beauty contest. It's not a boutique hot dog, but it is one serious little piece of meat in a bun."

At **Doogie's** in Newington, they will never tell you size doesn't matter. Franks here come by the foot. The waitress offers the "two-foot, all-the-way dog: chili, cheese, onions, peppers, and bacon."

Jane laughs. "They are almost obscene, this endless hot dog on this tiny little bun."

Meanwhile, at **Blackie's Hot Dog** stand in Cheshire, *Never on Fridays* might be the slogan. They're closed—going back to the days when Catholics couldn't eat meat on Fridays. Art Blackman opened Blackie's as a gas station in 1928, serving a few hot dogs on the side. Soon he was selling more hot dogs than gasoline, so he took out the pumps but kept selling franks. His relish is famous—its recipe a closely guarded secret.

For a gourmet experience alfresco, try the **Funki Munki** on Chapel Street in New Haven. Maurice Juarez used to serve *haute* cuisine at the Union League Café; now he serves *hot* dogs from a gleaming chrome cart just outside. Not only does the menu offer upscale toppings like mango habanero or a smoky chipotle sauce, but where else can you get a crème brûlée with your dog? Maurice garnishes each cardboard boat with a slice of watermelon, a mini pickle, and an itty-bitty pack

of Chiclets. And there's always Latin music, oldies, or Frank Sinatra on his boom box.

One happy customer says, "This is gourmet with a smile."

Just off I–95 in Norwalk is **Swanky Franks,** which Michael Stern calls "the quintessential road-house highway diner. It's so easy, it's right at the end of the exit ramp. The hot dogs are terrific. They are great, classic, deep-fried hot dogs. And the french fries are spectacular—just incredibly delicious."

Even when it's jammed, owner Bob Manere isn't flustered. His last job was as food service manager for the Pontiac Silverdome—where he fed eighty-eight thousand fans on game day. "You get people in here that come in with their last $2.20 and buy a hot dog, and then you get guys that pull in with their Rolls-Royces and Ferraris from Greenwich or Darien or New Canaan or Weston," he says. "We get customers from all walks of life. I guess the hot dog and french fry transcend economic lines."

Before the interstates were built, Bob adds, there were loads of little joints like his, selling hot dogs or seafood, but most of those have disappeared. That's why hot dog stands like these are remnants of our past—that never go out of style.

New Haven's Frostiest

The Puritans may have frowned on a lot of colonial pastimes, but drinking beer wasn't one of them, according to Amy Trout, curator of the New Haven Colony Historical Society. "The beer they drank was ale. It was a rich, hearty drink, dark in color and thick in body, and they made it themselves."

Later, in 1852, one Philip Fresenius went from making beer in washtubs and delivering it in kegs strapped to his back to opening one of the first and biggest breweries in New Haven. At its peak during the 1880s, the brewery produced one hundred thousand barrels of beer a year. "Industrialization, coupled with the new German immigrants who began to produce lager instead of ale, really changed the way Americans drank," says Amy, "as well as how Americans consumed beer, how they

bought beer, and how they thought about beer."

At one time there were more than twenty breweries in Connecticut, and most were in New Haven, where they made favorites such as Colonial Ale, Mule Head Wehle Ale, Holihan's Pilsner Beer, and Hull's Cream Ale. Most of them were shut down permanently by Prohibition during the 1920s.

"Later, some of them tried to start up again," Amy says. "Others had lost their fortune and simply went out of business. But the ones that started up again found tough times because they started up again in an economic depression in the 1930s. In New Haven," she adds wistfully, "most of them didn't survive."

And that's something we can all pause to regret as we pour the next tall frosty draft on a hot summer's day.

I Scream, You Scream, We All Scream...

On a steamy summer's day, could anything be as welcome as a scoop of sweet, cold, creamy ice cream? And the fresher, the better. Yankees are hard at work across our state to bring you summer refreshments, all bursting with the taste of Connecticut.

When you have the hot, humid summer blues and you need the cure—**Dr. Mike** has the prescription. His offices are in Bethel and Monroe in western Connecticut, and in summertime the doctor is in seven days a week. The ice cream that inspires such devotion has been singled out by *People* magazine as one of the top thirty ice creams in the nation. It's been called the best in the state by *Northeast, New England Monthly, Yankee,* and *Connecticut* magazines.

"Dr. Mike" is actually Robert Allison, an ice cream fanatic who has tried all the premium commercial brands. "Mine is far superior," he says. "They can't afford to use the level of mix we use—

16 percent butterfat or various cocoas from Holland or the true Madagascar pure vanilla."

When Robert bought Dr. Mike's from the artist who founded it, he increased production, but he says the secret to his top-of-the-line taste is "keep it small. . . . Ice cream tastes different as you make it in larger batches." Fresh cream delivered in ten-quart containers is the basic ingredient, and cashew, apricot, and banana walnut are among the 140 flavors he rotates. One of the biggest sellers, which is almost always available, features a candy made just down the road called Chocolate Lace. "Chocolate Lace is a very thin piece of caramel, covered in chocolate, broken up and stirred into

our ice cream." Voilà, Chocolate Lace and cream!

On a hot summer's night after supper there can be fifty people waiting in line in the parking lot, an informal ice cream social sponsored by the man they lovingly call "the ultimate dip," Dr. Mike.

Perching on a hay bale and licking a farm-made ice cream cone—what could be better on a sun-baked afternoon? Moving up the road to West Simsbury, the folks at **Tulmeadow Farm** produce thirty flavors, but on any given day they are scooping about sixteen. Still number one is vanilla, though plenty of people are partial to Don Tuller's signature flavor, red raspberry chocolate chip, made with an all-natural berry puree. Don has tried a number of new flavors since attending an ice-cream-making seminar at the University of Wisconsin not long ago. The most unusual one to come from that class: "Grape-Nuts with cinnamon and nutmeg." He's experimenting with a root-beer-flavored ice cream, and his double dark chocolate chip and mocha chip are enough to send some chocoholics into ecstasy. Tulmeadow Farm's store always offers at least one mint variety, though it might be mint chocolate chip one day, and mint brownie dough another.

Don doesn't mix too many doodads into his concoctions, saying with a chuckle, "I guess I am enough of a Yankee that I don't try to figure out how many expensive items I can add in and then charge the same as vanilla." He scoops from mid-April through the end of October, but pints and quarts are available year-round. Don is also known for his ice cream pies and ice cream sandwiches, which feature chocolate chip or Heath Bar cookies made at a local bakery as the crunchy outer layer.

In eastern Connecticut, folks living near the University of Connecticut campus in Storrs have enjoyed the frozen treat made in the university's own creamery from milk produced by the school's dairy herd since the 1950s. Now ice cream and Huskies fans all over the state can enjoy **UConn Dairy Bar Ice Cream,** because it's as close as their nearest supermarket.

The dairy bar continues to make and serve twenty flavors, but some old favorites like butter pecan and Jonathan's Supreme (vanilla ice cream with peanut butter swirls and chocolate-covered peanuts), as well as some new ones, are available in your local ice cream freezer as well. The signature flavor is a takeoff on one of the university's best-loved traditions, basketball season's Midnight

Madness. The chocolate ice cream is studded with orange malted milk balls resembling basketballs.

The university has long been known for its agricultural programs. "UConn has had a dairy herd since the beginning," says Dr. David Dzurec, an associate professor at the agricultural school. "It started out as the state's agricultural school, and it has kept that component."

All eight flavors come in half-gallon tubs, priced at $4.99 and decorated with the UConn Huskies mascot, the red Farwell barn, and other campus landmarks. The supermarket ice cream is a little richer than the ice cream served at the dairy bar, with 14 percent butterfat. Ten percent of ice cream royalties are donated to UConn. Cameron Faustman, head of the Animal Science Department, sees this "as a chance to raise some revenue in tough economic times, as well as highlight the university's agricultural studies programs." Adds Dr. Dzurec: "Ice cream has been a big part of the university and is one of its favorite products—along with our sports teams, of course!"

Down by Connecticut's waterside lie historic Old Lyme and its **Ice Cream Shoppe.** You might have some idea what Steve Albert misses most when he's called up to active duty in the Coast Guard Reserves: Mom, ice cream, and his favorite brew. That could be why Steve and his mother, Lou Mae Albert, opened their shop a few years ago and why Steve's most fabled creation is an ice cream he calls "Guinness," after the stout.

"That's really taking off," Lou Mae says. "It doesn't have any alcohol in it because it's boiled down, but it has the flavor for sure. You'd be surprised who comes in and orders it."

If you're thinking of minding your diet, the Alberts' slogan—stitched on aprons and T-shirts worn by the staff—may dissuade you: CARPE CRE-EM. Their ice creams are tempting, especially the seasonal flavors made with local produce like summer strawberry, native peach, and pumpkin. Among the other tastes that keep customers coming back are chocolate raspberry truffle, orange pineapple, and of course Guinness. The shop makes a variety of Italian ices, too—some of them in unusual flavors like granny apple, Bordeaux cherry, peach Melba, and strawberry kiwi.

Steve has been on active duty twice in the last couple of years. Apparently there's no special dispensation in the military for ice cream makers. As Lou Mae says, "We need him—this is our busy season!"

Shellfish Tales

My grandfather once told me he figured the first person to eat a clam or an oyster had to be either crazy or starving. Well, these days you don't have to be either to enjoy these delicacies—but it does help to be here in Connecticut.

At low tide in Guilford, not long after sunrise on an August morning, Chris Reaske has his clam rake in hand and is headed for the shore. He's been clamming for more than thirty years, and his success in and love for capturing steamers, quahogs, and littlenecks has resulted in a book titled *The Compleat Clammer*.

Some folks believe that all clams should be dug with the feet, Chris explains: "The Indians started that way, we know. And certainly primitive man did, too. It's called treading for clams when you use your feet. I myself am an advocate of wearing ratty old sneakers when you clam." On cold days he might pull on a pair of insulated boots.

Clamming, he continues, is really just a matter of timing. "If they had the choice, people historically have gone for clams before they've gone for fish, because clams are a sure thing," he says. "We know how the tides work, and we know how clams live and reproduce and where they are found." Get the timing right, he says, "and you can be pretty sure of success at it." If you are after soft-shell clams, usually called steamers, head to the mudflats at low tide; hard-shells are a little farther out. "I have actually clammed in water right up to my neck for the hard-shells we call quahogs," says Chris.

It doesn't take much equipment to get started. A clam rake with a built-in basket will dig and catch your hard-shell clams, a short-handled steamer rake or pointed shovel is a good idea, and you need a

bucket to hold several gallons of water, in which you deposit your catch to keep them alive. When I was a kid, we took a bushel basket, like the kind farmers use to gather peaches or apples, tucked it inside an inner tube that floated in the water, and tied it onto our bathing suits or belt loop on our shorts to keep the clams from drifting away.

When digging for clams you should check first with the Department of Environmental Protection, since some areas are occasionally closed to shellfishing because of pollution. You may also want to find out if you need a permit, whether there's a limit on how many clams you can take, and what size they must be to be legal.

What's the attraction of this pastime? "Our bodies are full of water and loaded with salt, and there are elements in our bodies that are almost the same as the elements in the oceans, in terms of minerals," Chris points out. "There's just a lot that keeps soulfully drawing us back to the sea. I know that when I am clamming, I feel as though I am being beckoned by that ancestral part of each of us."

When Hillard Bloom starting oystering, men in shallow-draft sailboats known as Sharpies still collected shellfish, and dozens of oyster companies dotted Connecticut's shoreline. "We dredged oysters under sail when we first got started," Hill recalled. "Then about 1955 or so, we started growing our own oysters," cultivating them on acres of beds in Long Island Sound.

In South Norwalk, Hillard Bloom Shellfish Inc.,

a family business, expanded as other oyster companies disappeared. "The hurricanes that started in 1939 and continued through the 1950s hurt the oyster business," Hill said. "We lost a lot of our inventory then. Of course, the pollution didn't help any." In the following years Hill Bloom saw overfishing cause a dramatic decline in oyster harvests, so he began clamming, too, dredging for littlenecks and cherrystones, and his company survived and thrived. Today Norwalk Bluepoints are considered among the best oysters in the country, with a nice hard shell, good fat meat, and a sweet taste.

Hill Bloom has passed away, but his family still harvests thousands of bushels of oysters from Long Island Sound yearly, shipping them all over the country. His kids have advanced the practices of cultivating shellfish, a process of underwater farming that goes back to the Native Americans who lived here hundreds of years ago. The Bloom shellfish company's new "hatchery" helps avoid some of the traditional difficulties of raising shellfish in the sound.

Captain Dave Hopp oversees a crew that works twelve hours a day, all year long. The grandson of an oysterman and the Blooms' cousin, Dave has been working the boats since he was fourteen years old, yet he has never lost his joy in life on the water. "The day goes fast," he says. "We have a lot of running time between one area and another, and that gives us time to just sit back and look at the scenery."

It's a good life, with a bounty of fresh summer shellfish we can all enjoy as reward.

BOUNTIFUL FARM STANDS AND FARMERS' MARKETS

CLOCKWISE FROM TOP LEFT: A COLORFUL ARRAY OF RADISHES; WELL-TENDED TRUCK IN WALLINGFORD; THIS ROADSIDE STAND ENTICES CUSTOMERS; FRAGRANT BOUQUET FROM CLINTON; WARM BREADS AT THE CHESTER FARMERS' MARKET; PINK MALVA BLOSSOMS ON THEIR WAY TO A STAND IN CLINTON. FACING PAGE: VEGGIES AND FARM-FRESH PRESERVES AT THE LYME FARMERS' MARKET.

A Taste of Summer

On the lawns of the Florence Griswold Museum, the Old Lyme Midsummer Festival takes place each year in late July or the first weekend of August. This open-air market is modeled after the ones dotting rural France, and some of the vendors have been moved by their visits to those markets. Stasia and Glenn Penkofflidbeck, for instance—who sell honey produced at their Three Sisters Farm in Essex—speak wistfully of the honey created by bees flying through fields of lavender in Provence.

"I grew up on a vegetable farm. My grandparents lived next door in Trumbull and they had apple trees. We had any kind of vegetables and fruit you can imagine," says Stasia. "So I grew up around bees. We had thirty hives. Then I went to school for zoology, and have a master's degree in that. This is something I always wanted to do."

Michael Newburg was on a different education path before founding **Falls Brook Organic Farm.** "I went to graduate school for anthropology, but I got burned out on graduate work," he says. "I noticed most of the space on my bookshelves was taken up by all these agricultural books, so I decided I should do it."

On the old Sterling and Harding homesteads in Lyme, which were settled in the late 1600s and farmed continuously until the 1930s, Michael harvests daily and will "pick to order." His wooden wine crates are brimming with arugula, heirloom lettuces like Amish Red Deer Tongue, and Caribe purple-skinned potatoes. His wife, Amelia Hunt, is selling table linens she imports from France.

Suzanne and Stan Sankow have been raising sheep at their **Beaver Brook Farm** in the Pleasant Valley section of Lyme since 1984 and recently added a few cows to their flock of six hundred sheep. Their popular sheep's milk feta is just one of the cheeses they make, including aged sheep's milk cheeses like Pleasant Valley and Farmstead as well as fresh cheeses such as their Summer Savory. Their Jersey cows' milk goes into their Camembert and Nehantic Abbey cheeses as well as yogurt and ice cream. Wares from their yarn shop are also for sale in their tent, including everything from fleece to sweaters. Business is brisk even on a hot August day, and shoppers are selecting lamb chops, rack of lamb, even lamb sausage. Chef Stuart London has created a gourmet food line at the farm, including a Bolog-

nese pasta sauce (lamb with fresh tomato, garlic, Chianti, and basil) and appetizer spreads. "The spreads are a creative way to do something with our low-fat sheep's milk ricotta," he says. "We have roasted garlic and sun-dried tomato, and a cheese and olive mixture made with three kinds of olives and two of our cheeses."

Allyn Brown, the owner of **Maple Lane Farms** in Preston, is quenching customers' thirst with his new black currant juice. The berry plants were banned in the United States for most of the 1900s because "it was an alternate host for a disease called white pine blister rust," says Allyn. Connecticut eventually

lifted the ban, and now Allyn is the largest grower of black currants in the country. "It's a great crop," he says, because "birds don't eat it, deer don't eat the plants, it doesn't get fungus, and we haven't needed pesticides, we just do a little weed control and that's it." The French have long been fond of the berry, making its rich juice into cassis.

Other tents offer artisan breads, freshly roasted coffee beans, hormone-free steaks, kettle corn, scones, and herbal teas. Even the birds will have something lovely to eat: Kids have gathered beneath the children's activity tent to craft birdseed cookies. Truly, a feast for all the senses!

FRESH FLAVORS IN CONNECTICUT

CLOCKWISE FROM TOP LEFT: ENJOYING U-LIK-IT ICE CREAM IN BROOKLYN; NORWALK OYSTER FESTIVAL; WATERMELON, A LATE SEASON FAVORITE; SAVORING STRAWBERRY SHORT-CAKE AT THE HAMBURG FAIR; TAKING TEA IN CHESTER; FARMSTAND-FRESH BERRIES; MANY FOODS TO SAMPLE AT WESTPORT'S ITALIAN FEST.

An Urban Oasis

Look closely in the heart of one of New Britain's oldest inner-city neighborhoods on a summer's day, and you'll spot a patch of green. City native Tony Norris runs Urban Oaks, a certified-organic farm that has transformed a neighborhood eyesore into an oasis.

Tony remembers a time before the site was run down and overgrown, when it was a wholesale florist known as Sandelli's. In those days a dozen greenhouses dotted both sides of the street, and people lined up to buy plants and flowers at the small retail shop. But Sandelli's had been closed for years when Tony Norris and John Nedosko took a look at the property in 1999. They got an eyeful, and it wasn't pretty.

"Everything was completely overgrown," John recalls. "There were trees growing out of the greenhouses. Everything that was inside was destroyed. There was no pane of glass unbroken, and there was trash and broken shards of pots all over."

Were they discouraged? "No," says Tony, laughing, "we were crazed!"

Tony and John—the head of the board of directors and another New Britain native—looked beyond what was there and saw what *could* be. "We could picture this because a lot of us are from New Britain. We remembered when Sandelli's was here and we would shop here," John says. "We never realized how much property there was. That was the biggest surprise. To our knowledge this is the only one like this in the country. It's been fun. It hasn't always been easy, but it's been fun."

They applied for some grant money to get going. Then they cleaned up the site, hauling away more than sixty dumptruck loads of trash. "The neighbors were elated," John says. "We had four volunteer cleanup nights and more than one hundred people each night, including the mayor." Volunteers are still showing up, too. "We had to cut a hole in the fence for our friend Anna Ruscito who lives next door. At five in the morning she comes

in to hoe," says Tony. "Not only does she *not* get paid but she comes by at least twice a week and feeds us lunch, like pasta with homemade ricotta."

In 1999 Urban Oaks opened as a certified-organic farm, growing herbs, salad greens, and vegetables inside six renovated greenhouses and in outdoor gardens on the rest of the three-acre site, which is surrounded by apartment buildings. Today Urban Oaks sells mostly wholesale, with restaurants and gourmet markets from Hartford to Westport clamoring for its produce. A tour of the greenhouse and gardens shows why. Where else can you find more than one hundred varieties of tomatoes growing, including dozens of heirlooms that were once nearly extinct? More than a dozen varieties of eggplant range from neon purple to orange. There are peppers called "fat 'n sassy," and purple Peruvian hot

peppers, and little ones that look like cheese wheels.

In one humid greenhouse there's flowering kale, chard, collard greens, Chinese cabbage, black cabbage, and parcel (a combination of parsley and celery). Another greenhouse is devoted to herbs, including rosemary, sage, lemongrass, lemon verbena, savory, Vietnamese cilantro, spiny Cuban cilantro, chives, and two dozen varieties of basil to complement dozens of world cuisines.

"We read seed catalogs like other people read literature," Tony says. "We get a really diverse and ethnic clientele who come here for things that aren't available anywhere else. In fact, at this point, when people go home to the old country, they bring us seeds." So the farm grows specialties like Middle Eastern purple Ararat basil and Santorini cherry tomatoes from Greece—but then a screech of tires from a drag race on Oak Street reminds us of the farm's urban location.

The National Organics Standards Board certifies the farm. That means it uses no synthetic materials in pesticides or herbicides and instead employs beneficial insects such as ladybugs or praying mantises to eat the pests. Some they pick off by hand, working "with nature, not against nature," according to Tony. Birds fly through the greenhouses and eat

bugs, and the farm is trying to attract bats, known for their voracious insect appetites.

On Thursday at midday the last wholesale orders go out and then the four part-timers and four full-timers start setting up for the farmers' market, held every Friday afternoon and Saturday morning year-round. (In early October it moves indoors.) Besides their own produce, the folks at Urban Oaks sell root crops from other organic Connecticut farms and natural meats from a farm in Vermont. They have organic tea and coffees, Connecticut maple syrup, and bakery products from Sweet Sage bakery.

John smiles. "It's become a gathering place where people show up on Saturday and get a scone and a coffee, meet friends, then do their shopping. Sometimes we get someone to come in and play guitar. It's a fun place." Urban Oaks Organic Farm is all that, and a summertime green oasis in the city, too.

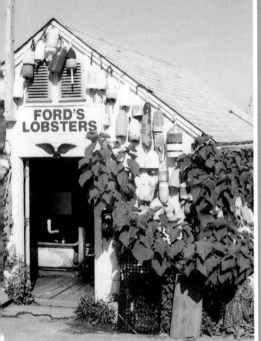

DINING ALFRESCO ON A SUMMER'S DAY

CLOCKWISE FROM TOP LEFT: LOBSTER IN THE ROUGH; STREETSIDE DINING AT CARSON'S IN NOANK; COLORFUL FURNISHINGS MAKE FOR FESTIVE OUTDOOR DINING AT THE BLUE OAR IN HADDAM; SEAFOOD COOKED OVER OPEN FLAME AT THE PLACE IN GUILFORD; THE PUMP HOUSE GRILL IN BUSHNELL PARK, HARTFORD; FORD'S LOBSTERS IN NOANK.

Lobster Lady

The name is emblazoned across the stern of her boat: *Andy's Girl.*

That's what most people called Vivian Volovar when she first started hanging out in boatyards. They all knew her dad, Andy. "He did his twenty years in the navy. He was a hard hat diver," says Vivian with quiet pride. "He built and repaired boats when he got out."

Most days from May through mid-September, and then again from Thanksgiving through the end of January, you'll find Vivian on her thirty-one-foot boat somewhere between the mouth of the Mystic River and Fishers Island, hauling her four hundred traps.

It's no wonder Vivian ended up spending her life on the water: She developed her sea legs around the time most kids are still negotiating a playpen. "When I was a kid, we'd be in the old life jackets strapped into the boat," she explains. "We had my second birthday out in the Race [a section of Long Island Sound] when my parents were bluefishing." Today Vivian is Connecticut's only licensed lobster woman. "You're watching and learning every day. I love it—I haven't had two days alike yet in twenty-five years of doing this."

She reaches into a barrel of bait, murmuring, "Five-month-old herring, nice and ripe, wonderfully aromatic!" That's Vivian's idea of understatement: The bait stinks, but the more "aromatic" the better, since lobsters are attracted by the smell of the herring Vivian places inside the trap. Inside is a complicated net web, and Vivian describes how it works. "They go in the front net forward to eat. When they're in there eating, somebody else comes for dinner, so they back up to defend themselves. They go up the back funnel backward. Once they get into a certain point, the horns on the top of their head get hung up on the funnels. They can't get out, so they have to fall into the pot."

But not every lobster is a keeper. Vivian is a stickler for measuring them. "First you check them to make sure they're a legal size," she explains and points to the one caught in the trap she has just hauled. "That one is short from the eye socket to the back of the main shell. It has to be a minimum of three and a quarter inches." Since it's not, she tosses it back into the water. Vivian also throws them back if the females are carrying eggs, or if she thinks they have one more breeding season left in them.

Undaunted by weather and hard labor and by a legal challenge, Vivian fought to continue to fish the waters around Fishers Island. The area is rich in lobsters as they migrate, so when the state of New York barred Connecticut residents from fishing there, Vivian went to court, and won.

"I don't have to fish long trawls anymore. I can get up in tight against the rocks and fish single pots, which are a lot easier for me," she says. "And I don't have to work in the boat traffic because farther out in the Sound in the summertime it's like being in the middle of an interstate highway."

Vivian relishes the solitude on her one-woman boat. She pooh-poohs the idea that the sea can be a dangerous place for a woman alone. "It's still safer than driving down that interstate. Out here it's me and the boat and the weather."

On a good day Vivian catches two or three hundred pounds of lobster, which she sells primarily to Abbott's in Noank. So after a long day on the boat, does she hurry home for a lobster dinner, maybe some lobster chowder? No way! She won't eat them, doesn't even like the smell of them.

Still, Vivian wouldn't trade the hard work of lobstering for any other job. "To me *hard* is having to be at work at nine o'clock, staying there and not being able to leave until the clock rings at four-thirty or five o'clock," she says. "I'd rather work from three or four in the morning till ten at night. At least I'm free."

Arts and Craftspeople

I have a secret. It's about summer camp. Sunny days learning to swim in the lake, starry nights around the campfire, telling ghost tales after lights out in our tent—they were all okay. But my favorite part of sleep-away camp, the hour I lived for each day, and endured all the rest for? Arts and crafts! Whether braiding a lanyard for a key ring for Mom, whipstitching a leather billfold that Dad would pretend to use, or crafting a clay mug so crooked it wouldn't hold coffee, arts and crafts was the session I yearned for. One summer, instead of camp, my mom signed me up for a class in creative writing. Other kids whined about the stuffy classroom, but I marveled at dust motes floating on sunbeams as I struggled to write short stories, essays, and poems. That class may have gotten me to this page today.

So the idea of spending a summer vacation working with a master textile artist like Ed Johnetta Miller, or learning to sing under the direction of the maestro of the Connecticut Opera—well, such opportunities make me long to be a child again and to take advantage of a summer that goes beyond lazing about the yard or heading for the beach. As an adult, I attend crafts festivals all over the state. I'm the one you'll find earnestly questioning the glass artist on just how he created a stenciled pattern between two layers of windowpane now forming a crenellated serving tray, or querying the woman turning postage stamps into brilliant designs for earrings.

The arts in Connecticut are among the best reasons to live here. Is classical music ever as fine as when heard outdoors at Harkness State Park beside a stately mansion, surrounded by formal gardens with the sea slapping the shore as an accompaniment? Or perhaps the sounds of Hot Steamed Jazz from New Orleans echoing through the Connecticut River Valley on a sultry summer night make you tap your toes. Have you been thrilled by the international array of artists of every stripe who annually descend upon New Haven for the two-week International Festival of Arts and Ideas? The Litchfield hills are alive with the sound of music—jazz, chamber, and classical—and in every corner of the state there are outdoor performances of music, poetry, and glorious theater, inspired by playwrights from Shakespeare to Connecticut's own brilliant bard, Eugene O'Neill.

Art and Soul

Ed Johnetta Miller's life is alive with rich hues and earthy textures that speak of summer in Connecticut. "This community has helped my career and has put me on the map as Ed Johnetta Miller, the international artist," she says. "It started right here in Hartford."

That may be why Ed Johnetta is always giving back to her community, though her career as a weaver, textile artist, and quilter has expanded globally. Her vibrant creations have been featured in magazines, on television, and in museums and galleries as far away as Africa, New Zealand, Australia, and Japan. Yet most days she can be found at the Hartford Artisan's Center, gently guiding older students in overcoming their disabilities by discovering their artistic talents.

Annie, an accomplished painter and writer, is learning to quilt. Ed Johnetta is clearly fond of her. "Annie is mesmerized by me and I am mesmerized by Annie. We have this mutual love thing going on. She becomes very angry because her sight is failing.

She said, 'I want to be young again.' But she has found a new life at the Artisan's Center, so I am hearing that frustration less and less. Now, it's more like, 'I love being here! I love the people here!'"

Ed Johnetta knows how that feels. She has overcome her own pain to continue the work that defines her. "I used to have severe arthritis, crippling arthritis, and I was worried because my hands started to change and my feet for my treadling and my sewing—it was, you know, almost unbearable for me," she recalls. "And I said, 'There has to be a better way.'"

Daily exercise and meditation have given her the strength and energy to maintain a schedule that often begins at five o'clock one morning and ends in her studio at one or two the next. And there may be one more element that keeps her going: a daily dose of love.

It comes quietly from an elderly weaving student at the Hebrew Home for the Aged. "Ed Johnetta, if it wasn't for you, I would not be so happy, because you are the one that has made my life full. Without you I'd be empty," proclaims Rose Michaelson.

Or it is expressed boldly with the enthusiasm of youth. Gathering around Ed Johnetta, schoolgirls point to a quilt they worked on together, shouting and pointing, "I did that one, I did that one." At the after-school program Girls Inc., Ed Johnetta shares more than her art with these girls; she also opens their eyes to the world beyond their neighborhood. "They're waiting for you, and they're so full of life and so eager to learn," she says, eyes shining. Her classes are always about more than artistic technique. "We share the fabric, we share the scissors,

and we are learning to communicate with one another and to be kind to one another," she reminds the girls gently.

Those are some of the same lessons she teaches to high school students from twenty-four Hartford-area towns as one of the master artists in the Greater Hartford Art Council's Neighborhood Studios program. For six weeks the ninety teens study at workshops in a variety of sites, from a rehearsal room at the Bushnell Theater to tents atop Hartford's Riverfront Plaza. Apprentices take classes in "Arts as a Profession" in the morning, and then work with master artists in public art, textiles, basket weaving, theater, music, and design. They hone their skills as young artists and learn the techniques needed to make a living making art. And Ed Johnetta believes there is a place for art in *every* life. "Each of us can learn how to take some of that stress and put it into a creative and more rewarding art form," she advises her students.

"Think of a way of taking negative force and putting it into something more positive."

En Plein Air

In the early decades of the twentieth century, the American impressionist painters found Florence Griswold's stately boardinghouse on the banks of the Lieutenant River in Old Lyme an inspiration for their canvases, many of which were painted *en plein air* or outdoors. On a sultry summer day about one hundred years after Childe Hassam helped establish Miss Florence's home as the Lyme Art Colony, a new crop of artists is clustered beneath the shade trees on the riverbank, outside the home that is now a museum.

Dick McEvoy, head of the Connecticut Pastel Society, is working on a landscape. "We went through the museum first to see all those wonderful people and their work"—many of the painters left their mark, literally, on Miss Griswold's walls and paneled doors. "It *is* very inspiring. But even without that"—he gestures to the riverscape before him—"*this* is inspiring. What a gorgeous day to sit in the shade and paint."

Ralph Schwartz and Susan Urquhart are standing in the footsteps of greats like Willard Metcalf and William Chadwick as they paint. "I am just a beginner and have never been here before," admits Susan, "but the history of this place is awesome."

ART AND ANTIQUING ON A SUNNY WEEKEND

TOP ROW: COLLECTIBLES AT A FLEA MARKET IN WESTBROOK AND WHIMSICAL GOBLETS AT THE GUILFORD HANDCRAFTS FAIR; CENTER: ONE OF THE MANY ANTIQUES STORES IN EAST HADDAM; BOTTOM ROW: AN ARTIST DISPLAYS HER JEWELRY AT THE GUILFORD HANDCRAFTS FAIR; CHOICE FURNISHINGS AT THE FARMINGTON VALLEY ANTIQUES FAIR HELD OUTDOORS AT THE POLO GROUNDS IN FARMINGTON.

Hometown Boy

A wood-paneled room in a New London summer cottage is more than the setting for two great American plays; it's also the setting for the real life of playwright Eugene O'Neill, the only American playwright to win a Nobel Prize.

Both *Ah, Wilderness!*—O'Neill's only comedy—and the tragic *Long Day's Journey into Night* play out against the backdrop of Connecticut's Monte Cristo Cottage.

Famed nineteenth-century actor James O'Neill bought the summer house on the Thames River in 1888 and named it Monte Cristo Cottage after his most famous role, the Count of Monte Cristo. Since the family traveled with O'Neill's acting company the rest of the year, this was the only home the O'Neill children knew in their early lives. Young Eugene and his siblings lived here at a time when New Londoners all turned out on the Fourth of July for fireworks and fun—much as they did in *Ah, Wilderness!*

It was the era of bathing costumes and ragtime, but it had a darker side—the rise of industrial mills,

child labor, and what O'Neill called the "underclass." Sally Paretti, curator of the Monte Cristo Cottage, explains that the O'Neills were not immune to their age. The home held many secrets—secrets about a mother's drug addiction and about a brother's alcoholism—agonizing secrets that O'Neill revealed in his masterpiece *Long Day's Journey.* "He didn't want the play published for twenty-five years after his death so that all of those New London friends of his would have passed away," Sally notes. "Anybody who knew the O'Neill family would have been long gone, so it wouldn't make any difference." But Eugene O'Neill's third wife, Carlotta Monterey O'Neill, sold the play just two years after his death, lifting the veil over the life in Monte Cristo Cottage.

Today the summer home is a museum that details O'Neill's times and talent. It's part of the

LEFT: AMANDA MADDOCK'S *BUILD A BETTER BOWER* AT THE O'NEILL PUPPETRY CONFERENCE. TOP RIGHT: LLOYD RICHARDS AND MICHAEL DOUGLAS AT THE O'NEILL PLAYWRIGHTS CONFERENCE. BOTTOM RIGHT: AL PACINO IN ISRAEL HOROVITZ'S *THE INDIAN WANTS THE BRONX* AT THE PLAYWRIGHTS CONFERENCE. BELOW: MONTE CRISTO COTTAGE. FACING PAGE: SEANA KOEFOED AND KATHERINE POWELL IN LISA DILLMAN'S *ROCK SHORE,* PLAYWRIGHTS CONFERENCE.

Eugene O'Neill Theater Center in nearby Waterford, where in summer you can watch plays, musicals, and cabaret acts born right in front of your eyes. Actors often work with script in hand, using minimal props, costumes, and sets. For thirty years the O'Neill Playwrights Conference, Music Theater Conference, Puppetry Conference, National Theater Institute, and Critics Institute has nurtured writers and directors, puppeteers, actors, and singers as they create new work, which has gone on to Broadway, regional theater, the movies, and TV. More than seven hundred plays and musicals have premiered at the O'Neill, including John Guare's *The House of Blue Leaves,* August Wilson's *Ma Rainey's Black Bottom* and *The Piano Lesson,* Lee Blessing's *A Walk in the Woods,* and *Nine* by Arthur Kopit, Mario Fratti, and Maury Yeston.

Years after his death, Eugene O'Neill's life and work continue to inspire those who flock to his old hometown.

A Paradise for Poetry

oet Galway Kinnell once called the Hill-Stead estate's Sunken Garden a "little paradise for poetry," and so it has been for more than a dozen years, as the setting for the Sunken Garden Poetry Festival. The grand home's pioneering female architect and eventual owner Theodate Pope Riddle would have loved that, since the space, created by noted garden designer Beatrix Farrand around 1920, often hosted Theodate's many fascinating and accomplished guests, including the great novelist Henry James (who once called Hill-Stead "an exquisite palace of peace, light and harmony"), writers Sinclair Lewis and Thornton Wilder, artist Mary Cassatt, and First Lady Eleanor Roosevelt. Now thousands more enjoy the charms of the 152-acre hilltop estate in Farmington each summer, gathering on lawn chairs and blankets in and around the garden to hear poetry and music. Poet Naomi Ayala described the experience this way: "I've read in every environment you can imagine, but the Sunken Garden is an appropriate place for poetry—the way your words hang in the air there." Other poets who have shared their gifts to the rapt crowd include Pulitzer Prize–winner Maxine Kumin and national poet laureate Billy Collins. One night each season is dedicated to the winners of a statewide poetry competition for high school students.

The poetry is paired with music—which might range from a swing band to the sounds of a single flute lilting over Hill-Stead's stone walls and meadows. The home, a National Historic Landmark, is open before the performances for a self-guided tour, and its wonderful collection of paintings by Monet, Degas, Manet, Cassatt, and Whistler are alone worth the price of admission. Picnic suppers are available. The six biweekly poetry and music performances feature world-class and emerging poets from June through August, the verses blooming along with the blossoms.

Strawhat and Beyond

Filled with pastoral beauty and open spaces, yet only the proverbial stone's throw from the bright lights of Broadway, Connecticut has not surprisingly enjoyed a long tradition of high-quality summer theater. And venues across the state continue that tradition today—while often expanding it into year-round productions.

When the **Ivoryton Playhouse** in Essex opened in June 1930, it became the first self-supporting summer theater in the nation. Others are older, but are supported by foundations or wealthy families.

In 1908 the building was the recreation hall for the employees of the Comstock-Cheney factory, which turned out items made from ivory, most notably combs. When the company closed, the building probably would have been razed—had it not been for Milton Stiefel. An actor, Milton went on to become an assistant director to the "Bishop of Broadway," theater impresario David Belasco, and then signed on as manager and stage director for many productions that traveled nationally. He retreated to Essex following one of these tours to rest and recuperate. That's when he spotted the recreation hall and decided to recruit a company of resident players to perform there all summer. The actors lived in town and borrowed most of the stage props from their rented houses. As the reputation of the theater grew, actors vied to appear at the playhouse, including Katharine Hepburn, Art Carney, Kim Hunter, Marlon Brando, Shelley Winters, Tallulah Bankhead, Lillian Gish, Joan Bennett, Sid Caesar, Mae West, Alan Alda, and more.

The theater went dark during World War II when rationing gasoline and tires made it difficult for audiences to get to Ivoryton, but after the war Stiefel reopened and the cavalcade of stars continued. Another owner purchased the playhouse in the early 1970s when Stiefel retired but had a hard time making a go of it, and the historic playhouse was in danger of closing to make room for a drugstore. That's when the nonprofit Ivoryton Playhouse

Foundation was formed to save the landmark. The theater is still active all summer, and stages some events throughout the year.

Its resident company, the River Rep, presents revivals and new work. In 2003 the playhouse staged the world premiere of *A Woman of a Certain Age,* a musical based loosely on the life of an area resident, Florence Griswold. In real life Miss Florence, as she was known, turned her home into a boardinghouse for American impressionist artists in Old Lyme. The musical is set in modern times, but oral histories uncovered at the Florence Griswold Museum played a part in shaping the story. Its three local collaborators, Colin McEnroe, Steve Metcalf, and Lary Bloom, intended to present a staged reading of the work, but as Colin told the audience before one performance, "We underestimated the enthusiasm that

Ivoryton can bring to a project." Soon *A Woman of a Certain Age* was a full-blown stage production.

"This is a lovely way to spend an evening," croons Natalie Cole as she strides around the circular stage at the **Oakdale Theater.** For nearly five decades this has been a lovely way to spend a summer evening, since Ben Siegel first pitched his tent in Wallingford. The year was 1954 and the site was an alfalfa field. When Hurricane Carol flattened that tent on the last day of August that summer, Ben and his family sewed the shredded canvas back together, only to have it knocked down again two weeks later by Hurricane Edna. Undaunted, Ben put the tent right back up again.

In its earliest days the Oakdale Theater presented musicals, and it was the first time many customers had seen a live stage production. Ben remembered the man who came up to him on his first visit to the theater and asked, "So when do you run the newsreel?"

"They soon discovered we speak English, we sing, we dance, we tell stories," Ben chuckled. "And it worked." Musical theater was a natural for Ben. He'd spent ten years as managing director of the Shubert Theater in New Haven, where many shows debuted before they went to Broadway.

In 1972 the big top tent was replaced by a wooden dome and theater in the round, though it remained open air on the sides. Musical theater gave way to pop, rock, and country acts like Tom Jones, Harry Belafonte, Liberace, Diana Ross, Cream, The Who, and The Doors. Throughout the decades, "Anybody who is anybody has played here," boasted Ben, and he was right.

Sadly, Ben passed away in 2003. His legacy remains, however. Now owned by Clear Channel, the new year-round Oakdale Theater presents Broadway shows again, as well as dance and musical performances of all kinds. It's still located on the same site in Wallingford.

If a star turn by Leonardo DiCaprio in *Romeo and Juliet* doesn't turn kids on to Shakespeare, maybe this performance of *Twelfth Night* will. "Are thou not the Lady Olivia's fool?" comes the voice from the stage under a canopy of trees.

Jason Velasquez, a New Haven teen, was skeptical. "I thought that would just be boring, that there was no action, no fun in it, just all these funny words."

Then the high school sophomore was introduced to Shakespeare by working with the **Elm Shakespeare Company** one recent summer. Now, he admits, "it's a lot better than I thought! Shakespeare can be funny, it can be dramatic, it can be whatever you really want. That really surprised me."

Artistic director James Andreassi helped found Elm Shakespeare in 1995, and continues to direct its students and theater professionals. He remembers that in its first year, thirty-five hundred people came to see the free production in New Haven's Edgerton Park. Today audiences have grown to nearly thirty thousand a season, and the troupe performs in both New Haven and on the Guilford green. An actor himself, Jim says, "It seemed important that people be exposed not only to the theater but to the power and magic of Shakespeare's words, the plays."

Along the way they learn other things, too, like how a team works together. "Audiences think that the play just happens, but there's an incredible number of people who are doing a myriad of different tasks to make a performance happen," Jim explains. The nonprofit company offers artist-in-residency programs at New Haven schools and intensive summer internship programs in theater crafts, in which students mix with theater professionals at every level.

Although John Hadden has performed on stage, on TV, and in film, he still gets a kick out of introducing audiences old and young to the Bard. In this production he plays Feste. He hopes the crowds leave the show with "a twinkle in their eye and a feeling that I didn't get that when I went to the library to read the play."

How does a theater in a creaky 168-year-old barn attract a superstar like Paul Newman to perform in *Our Town*? It helps if the artistic director of the theater is Newman's wife, Joanne Woodward. The actress took the reins of the **Westport Country Playhouse** in 2000. She not only saved the beloved old theater from collapse, but also launched a twenty-two-million-dollar fund-raising campaign to renovate the red barn, known for its church pew seats and its history as a place where some great plays have opened and some big stars have gotten their starts. In 1940, when Westport summer resident and composer Richard Rodgers attended a performance of *Green Grow the Lilacs*, he mused that it might make a good musical, and three years later *Oklahoma!* opened on Broadway. Liza Minelli and Jane Fonda got their starts on stage here.

But Joanne Woodward has not concentrated solely on the theater's physical needs. She has fed the soul of its audience, too, bringing major stars into the theater for revivals, such as Richard Dreyfuss in

LISA BOSTNAR AND TWO ELM SCHOLAR INTERNS AT ELM SHAKESPEARE COMPANY.

Arthur Miller's *All My Sons*. Woodward has also nurtured new works, including a recent production of *The Good German* directed by Tony Award–winning actor and director James Naughton. David Wiltse, a resident of Weston, where Naughton also makes his home, wrote the play. Set against the backdrop of the Holocaust, it's not the kind of light work many people associate with summer theater. Still , James says, "There are audiences for substantive material. I'd much rather go to a play that is stimulating intellectually and emotionally, and about something that is important. Last year Westport did a production of *Master Harold and the Boys*—Athol Fugard's exploration of bigotry in South Africa. We didn't know if we would have an audience for it. We were really heartened to see that the community embraced the production."

Beginning in 2005, its seventy-fifth anniversary season, the Westport Country Playhouse will offer theater year-round in its refurbished home, thanks to Joanne Woodward and a lot of other actors who cared about preserving a tradition.

Little Divas

The lives of little girls in the inner city may contain drama, but it's not often accompanied by the majesty of opera unless they "Take Center Stage." That's the name of a three-week workshop held in Hartford co-sponsored by the Connecticut Opera and the Salvation Army.

Nine-year-old Bria Scott is enrolled for the third straight year, though she's modest about her singing voice. "It's okay—not that great, though. I like the opera and I like to dance and sing. We do lots of creative things and it's fun."

And that's the key to getting children to fall in love with opera, according to Connecticut Opera maestro Willie Anthony Waters, who is always reaching out to the community in innovative ways. "Not only are we finding a new audience for opera, but we might find some homegrown talent," he says. "The whole idea is not to make them into opera singers," admits Willie. "It's to open up opportunities for them so they can use whatever talents they have to enjoy themselves and then enjoy some of the finer things in life."

The girls participate in vocal training, stagecraft, dance and movement, and scenery and costume design, under the coaching of Mary Fox, a public school music teacher and opera singer. Mary believes that while the children are not familiar with the language or the music, they are open to the sound of opera. The maestro, who steps in for a class in conducting, says today's kids are primed and ready for opera, because they grew up with music videos on channels like MTV.

"They show videos that have stories and costumes and it's staged," he says. "We take it from there. These kids are exposed to that all the time. We amplify that, but we use operatic topics instead of whatever else they do on MTV."

These little divas are embracing words and glorious music—and an expanding horizon.

SOUNDS OF MUSIC

CLOCKWISE FROM TOP LEFT: NEW HAVEN
METROPOLITAN OPERA ON THE GREEN;
PICNICKERS AND PERFORMERS ON THE
GROUNDS OF THE NORFOLK CHAMBER
MUSIC FESTIVAL; HOT STEAMED JAZZ FESTI-
VAL IN ESSEX; THE COAST GUARD BAND AT
WADSWORTH MANSION IN MIDDLETOWN.

Tanglewood in Connecticut

The skies are gray and a little threatening for this performance of the Hartford Symphony under the stars at the Talcott Mountain Music Festival, but at the symphony's summer home in Simsbury the weather isn't dampening the spirits of music lovers.

Tonight Big Bad Voodoo Daddy—a swing band with a cool reputation and a hot new CD that premiered the night before on Jay Leno's show—will join the orchestra. The crowd, seated at tables and on the lawn, has been encouraged to dress and picnic in the spirit of the swing era. There are young women in polka-dot dance frocks and men decked out in zoot suits.

Some picnickers have decorated with themes, including "Putting on the Ritz" (feather boas and tiaras) and "Island Swing" (golfers from a local country club outfitted with leis and pink flamingos). Another table is a profusion of vines, Hawaiian flowers, and a hula girl amid platters of shrimp, oysters, and crab legs complemented by chilled bottles of Chardonnay.

Janet Keough of East Granby is judging the table contest. "We wanted people to come up with anything from the swing era. Our prizes are for most patriotic, most creative, and most elaborate."

Susan Suprenant is clearly in contention for the most elaborate award. Dubbed the Martha Stewart of South Windsor, she's topped her table with an antique lace cloth, gold-rimmed china, and silver flatware. Completing the elegant scene are sage-colored votive candles and matching tapers in crystal candlesticks, while tiny antique bottles at each place hold buds from Susan's garden. Her guests are helping themselves from a three-tiered antique silver plate to filo wrapped around feta and kalamata olive custard, egg rolls, and turkey, ham, spinach, and red pepper swirls.

On the lawn, other picnics range from pizza and beer to a family seated on a checked tablecloth, sipping champagne and lighting candles on a four-foot-tall candelabra.

As the skies darken the symphony takes to the stage in summer formalwear and plays "Summertime" from George Gershwin's *Porgy and Bess*. Then Big Bad Voodoo Daddy comes thundering on stage with its horns and its trademark song: "You and Me and the Bottle Makes Three." Scotty Morris leads the musicians and the crowd in the classic he calls "the first million seller. From 1933—it's 'Minnie the Moocher' by the great Cab Calloway!" The audience delights in the shout-and-response chorus "hi de hi de hi de hi," and people get up to dance. Some are newcomers to big-band music; others remember it from its heyday in their youth.

"It's pretty exciting to come in with a band and then work this stuff out and watch it develop," says musician Scotty Morris. "The great thing about this kind of music is that it's live and you never know what's going to happen night to night. And nothing is better than playing outdoors."

As for playing along with the Hartford Symphony Orchestra, Scotty comments: "It's like driving a big old 1940s Cadillac—it's pretty awesome. Once it gets going there's no stopping it!"

And on this night, there's no stopping the pleasure of the crowd. Even when raindrops start falling, umbrellas open and sway to the music. It is, after all, summertime in Simsbury at the Talcott Mountain Music Festival.

Isle of Inspiration

Art that inspires and tells a story: That is the sacred art of the great churches and cathedrals. Some of the world's best-known masterpieces were created for patrons within the Catholic Church.

Today sacred art finds its inspiration in the atmosphere of faith and the beauty of an island off the coast of Mystic. Twelve-acre Enders Island is home to St. Edmund's Retreat and the St. Michael Institute of Sacred Art, where retreats and classes in the sacred arts are offered year-round. But no season is as popular as summer, when the island's gardens are in bloom and when sailboats glide past the island on their way to and from Long Island Sound.

"There's a stream of tradition that runs from the time of the Apostles right up until the present day that's reflected in the art of the church, the Catholic Church, and also the Christian community in general," says Mark Gordon, the director of operations at St. Edmund's Retreat during the time of my visit.

"People remark that there is a lot of grace on Enders Island," Mark continues. "Not only do you encounter the beauty of God's natural creation, but

there's a spirit here among the staff, among the volunteers, benefactors, our friends, and our retreatants, that makes it a very special place." That spirit is present for guests who stroll the paths through formal gardens or bring a beachcomber's treasures of shells and stones to the open-air chapel. There are moments of solitude looking out on the sea, and views of three states.

From the 1920s until 1954, the island was the gracious home of Dr. Thomas Enders and his wife, Alyce. A devout Presbyterian, Alyce Enders found "much evidence of God" in this special place, and when she died she wanted the island to go to the church. The Presbyterian Church was not prepared to take it over, so Alyce donated Enders Island to the Society of St. Edmund as a place where priests and brothers could take their early education, known as formation. When religious vocations dwindled around 1980, the order looked for other ways to support the island and opened up the mansion and guest houses for religious retreats.

Marie Cox has come from New Haven several times to experience the retreats. "The spirituality here, the closeness to God, the removal. We're actually two islands off the mainland—you have to go from one island and then to this island to get here. It removes from your life the distractions that keep you away from God. When I come here, I look forward to that time alone with God."

In 1998 Mark, a recent convert to the Catholic Church, was looking for ways to expand St. Edmund's mission of evangelism and spiritual renewal. "I was charged with trying to find additional avenues of ministry that could help support St. Edmund's Retreat financially. What we decided

Jesus falls the third time.

was to capitalize on our long history of the arts here on Enders Island."

Dr. Thomas Enders had been an artist, and what is now the chapel was originally his art studio. The St. Michael Institute of Art was born, teaching the fine arts nurtured in the church, from woodcarving to fresco painting, iconography, manuscript illumination, and stained-glass design.

The faculty is made up of specialists from around the world. Nick Parrendo, a master artist from Pittsburgh, teaches a weeklong course on stained glass for beginners and more advanced students. "We go into scripture and we can find all that we want to do, to see how God is revealed to us, so that we can illustrate it," explains Nick.

Ed Harfmann, a painter from Queens, came here to work on his first stained-glass project. "Because of the quiet and the peaceful surroundings you get to hear the still small voice from within," he says softly. "In the outside world you don't get to hear that still small voice because the sound drowns it out, but here the environment definitely adds to it."

And Ed found a community of support. "I learned we're not an island unto ourselves, even though we are right now on Enders Island."

Recently a new chapel was completed. The artwork inside was done by the instructors who teach on the island.

Non-Catholics are invited to join the retreats, conferences, and classes offered on Enders Island, and some ten thousand people a year find renewal here. "We offer a universal experience," says Mark, "so that people would come here Catholic, non-Catholic, non-Christian, and leave with a wonderful sense of holiness and wholeness."

Family Fare

Summer starts for me with a parade marking Memorial Day. My favorites are the parades in small towns across Connecticut, featuring fire engines, handcrafted floats, and kids riding bikes with red, white, and blue streamers laced through the spokes of the wheels. Those parades remind me of the ones that used to mark the season on Long Island, where my grandparents spent their summers escaping the heat of Brooklyn for the sea breezes. I still get a thrill and find myself marching in place as the band strikes up its first notes and the grand marshal steps off on the parade route. As one of five children growing up in New York City, my earliest summers meant heading for the country, often to my grandmother's bungalow on the Great South Bay (which my dad built with his own hands as a teenager). We spent our days clamming, crabbing, and boating. Then there was our yearly excursion to the Adirondack Mountains for two weeks on the shores of Lake George, swimming, waterskiing, and visiting places like Catskill Game Farm or Fort Ticonderoga. When our family moved to the suburbs, we loved playing outside until dark and catching fireflies in old jelly jars with holes poked in the lids.

Our parents taught us to appreciate what is right in our backyard, which probably led to my penchant for exploring every corner of my adopted home, Connecticut. That's why I traveled the carousel trail, finding magical horses and beasts to whirl upon, or wondered at the actor who called a castle high above the river his summer cottage. The same curiosity has led me to museums of every sort—ones dedicated to time, to trucking, even to the history of firefighting.

Carnival midways with Ferris wheels and scary rides still beckon, with their sweet cotton candy and games of chance. Yet they're just one aspect of many of the agricultural fairs in our state, where we can also admire the 4-H projects of children raising chickens that look like exotic peacocks, or sheep that are fuzzy and fat, and as well groomed as any city matron's prized poodle. With their giant zucchinis and homemade jams, the fairs are perhaps our best bridge to the past, when Connecticut was a place where a small town was a destination, while the farmlands were our heart and soul and source of survival.

Paying Tribute

Norwalk is one of the biggest cities in Connecticut, but its riverfront village of Rowayton has all the charm of any of our state's tiniest towns.

And it is never more apparent than on Memorial Day weekend, when all of Rowayton turns out for an old-fashioned hometown parade.

From the lemonade stand manned by three little kids (with proceeds going to a Connecticut-based worldwide charity) to the strawberry shortcake served after the festivities on the grounds of one of the most historic homes in town, this is pure Americana. Even cloudy and cool weather on a day that's traditionally considered the start of summer doesn't discourage the crowds from gathering, decked out in sweaters and sweatshirts of red, white, and blue stars and stripes. Hannah and Emmet Towey—four and a half and two and a half years old, respectively—wave their flags as their mom, Andrea, pulls them along the parade route in an old-fashioned little red wagon.

Jack Raymond is the chief engineer of the Rowayton Fire Department, and he's driving a 1951 Mack pumper, one of five fire rigs in the parade. "These are all working rigs," Jack says. "Even this old gal would come out if we needed her."

Seated beside him, proudly wearing a fire department cap, is his seven-year-old daughter Jenny. Some of the fire company marches on foot towing a 1902 hose assembly behind them, one last remnant of the year the hose company was founded.

They are followed by a cadre of antique cars, including a gleaming Model A, an award-winning marching band from the Norwalk's Brien McMahon High School, the Nash Engineering Company band, the Roton Middle School marching band and color guard, the Cub Scouts, the Brownies, the Little League, a parade of pooches, and Michael Siek riding the village's only Segway.

Then the crowd clusters around an ancient cannon on the green, now decked out with red, white, and blue bunting, as the mayor and other dignitaries gather to speak and mark the occasion with a remembrance of all veterans who have given their lives.

Douglas Bora, a highly decorated World War II veteran, carries the wreath made by his sister-in-law Jane "Putsie" Richey, in memory of her father, a World War I navy vet. Putsie has created and donated a wreath each of the thirty-four years the parade has been held, and Douglas Bora has marched in each parade. At seventy-nine he still fits into his old army uniform, though he confides, "I can't exhale or I might pop a button." This year Doug has decided an old tradition from his childhood must be revived, and he recites a portion of Abraham Lincoln's Gettysburg Address: "Four score and seven years ago our fathers brought forth, upon this continent, a new nation, conceived in liberty, and dedicated to the proposition that all men are created equal."

He concludes with these words: "That we here highly resolve these dead shall not have died in vain; that the nation, shall have a new birth of freedom, and that government of the people by the people for the people, shall not perish from the earth."

As eleven-year-old Levon Ofgang plays a haunting solo of "Amazing Grace" on the bagpipes, the wreath is laid at the cannon's granite base. Two Blackhawk helicopters from the Connecticut National Guard fly over as the crowd joins Judy Livingston in singing "America the Beautiful," just as she has each Memorial Day for nearly twenty years. As the solemn ceremony ends, some wipe away a tear before heading for Pinkney Park for strawberry shortcake and the start of another Rowayton summer.

I Love a Parade

What could be more emblematic of Independence Day than a parade? The Barnum Festival's **Wing Ding Parade** is held every June in Bridgeport, just outside the entrance to Connecticut's Beardsley Zoo. It's part of the Barnum Festival, a thirty-day-long Fourth of July celebration inspired by the circus impresario, showman, and former Bridgeport resident and mayor P. T. Barnum, whose birthday happened to be July 5. Founded in 1949 as a way to raise the spirits post–World War II, the event was dubbed the Wing Ding Parade because it's the afternoon when children have a wingding of a time, enjoying the antics of clowns, games, face painting, and food. For the crowd that gathers, the highlight is seeing the kids themselves,

who are decked out in homemade costumes and adorn their bikes or wagons with festive flags, streamers, and balloons.

Six-year-old Janice Cancel of Bridgeport is dressed as the Chiquita Banana Lady. "I'm wearing a dress from Puerto Rico and my mother helped me make it. We bought fruit and tried to decorate it," Janice explains. Red plastic grape earrings dangle from her ears, and an Easter basket turned upside down and wired with fake fruit serves as her headdress. Janice doesn't even mind the wiring wrapped around her ears to secure the basket. She's just eager to step off and march.

All heads turn as the Dominican Artistic and Cultural Youth Group of Bridgeport dances by. Their red, white, and blue costumes flow gracefully as they take command of the street during their performance. Some of their full skirts are sewn from American and Connecticut flags

The festival's newly named mascot, Spirit the Elephant, is embodied by thirty-three-year-old Lori Pecorelli. "It's all about family, friends, and fun for all ages," Lori says. It is, and it's more than a little bit about tourism, too: The Barnum Festival was honored with the 2003 Spirit of Connecticut Award for its contributions to the state. The monthlong calendar of events includes concerts, fireworks, and an exotic car show and attracts about two hundred thousand people from as far away as California and Montreal, mak-

ing it one of New England's biggest festivals. Still, it's the intimacy, the excitement on the faces of kids, and the innocence of the Wing Ding that make this parade so special.

But it's not the only parade Connecticut has to offer. How about one where *everyone* is encouraged to march? You don't have to play an instrument to join the three thousand marchers in Willimantic. All you have to play is a radio.

The **WILI Boom Box Parade** was the 1986 brainchild of the late Kathy Clark. Budget cuts meant the town had lost its high school marching band, and Kathy and a few friends came up with the idea of canned music—Sousa marches and all—played on a local radio station and broadcast by marchers and spectators tuned in on their boom boxes. WILI radio host Wayne Norman embraced the idea, and the station has provided the soundtrack ever since.

Wayne leads the parade each year as grand marshal. He has been known to don boom box shoes as part of his natty attire, or in-line skate the length of the parade pulling a bus-sized boom box behind him, or drag a dogsled with the UConn Huskies mascot aboard while he shoots hoops through a basketball net attached to the back of one of his radio colleagues.

Tara Risley, the program coordinator of the Town of Windham Recreation Department, says the parade has become "humongous, with three thousand marchers and at least fifteen thousand spectators—which is just about equal to the population of Willimantic. The route is a mile long, the procession takes nearly two hours, and people are standing forty deep in some places. It's insane."

"No matter who you are," adds Grand Marshal Wayne, "you are welcome in our parade."

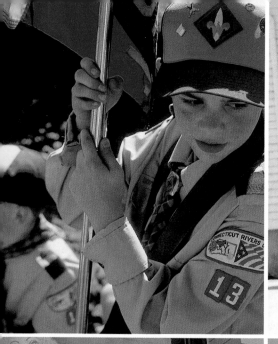

THREE CHEERS FOR THE RED, WHITE, AND BLUE!

CLOCKWISE FROM TOP LEFT: BOY SCOUTS AT THE MEMORIAL DAY PARADE IN CHESTER; PROUD TO BE AN AMERICAN AT THE EAST WOODSTOCK FOURTH OF JULY JAMBOREE; A PATRIOTIC CAKE FOR A FOURTH OF JULY CELEBRATION AT HARKNESS MEMORIAL STATE PARK IN WATERFORD; FLAG WAVING IN WILLIMANTIC; FLAGS SNAP IN THE BREEZE IN WESTPORT; WEARING "PARTY LIPS" IN DOWNTOWN MYSTIC.

Gillette's Legacy

One of the most colorful of Connecticut's sons, William Hooker Gillette, is remembered and celebrated today both on stage and in his unusual home, Gillette Castle.

Born in 1855 to Francis Gillette (a U.S. senator) and Elizabeth Hooker Gillette (whose relative, Thomas Hooker, was the founder of Hartford), William was perhaps the most famous actor of his day, and the man who made *Sherlock Holmes* a household word in this country.

"When he was in his late forties he met a man named Sir Arthur Conan Doyle, the British author of the Sherlock Holmes stories," explains Whitney Sternberg, a tour guide to Gillette's home. "Gillette asked to turn them into plays and Sir Arthur Conan Doyle told him to go ahead, because he was so tired of Sherlock Holmes he didn't want to have to write the stories anymore. And he never even asked for royalties from the plays, which was his loss, because Gillette made over three million dollars in his lifetime and performed in thirteen hundred performances over thirty-four years."

These days, of course, Gillette's acting chops are overshadowed by his home—famed Gillette Castle that towers over East Haddam and reveals even more facets of its legendary creator. It was at the height of his fame, in 1913, that Gillette decided to build his retirement home on the hill. Beginning in 1914, it took twenty men five years to construct the basic structure, and another seven years to complete it at a cost of nearly a million dollars. Still, as a widower with no children, Gillette never really retired from the stage or from touring; he ultimately spent only a few weeks a year on his 184-acre estate, which he knew as the "Seventh Sister"—named after the hill on which it was perched, one of a chain of seven mounts with majestic views of the Connecticut River.

Recently the state of Connecticut undertook a massive restoration of the castle and its surrounding

parkland. The project—which required eleven million dollars and about eighteen months—has left the home even more clearly a monument to Gillette's broad creative genius. "He wanted it to look like a ruin on the Rhine," says Linda Levine of the Department of Environmental Protection, who served as renovation supervisor, "and I think he accomplished that."

The castle's irregular fieldstone facade (it tops a steel structure) was leaking and cracking, and stonemasons labored over it. The roof was replaced, as were stone walls leading up the driveway, walkways, and parapets. "Grand Central Station," as Gillette called the terminal point for his three-mile-long narrow-gauge railroad, has been reinforced, and the carved cats on its roof replaced. But the real changes are noticeable inside the castle, where Gillette's quirky and creative interior has regained its original rustic feeling and luster.

All the furnishings have been reupholstered, and there has been intricate refurbishing of the raffia wall covering. "For years they looked like simply a straw color, but when they were taken down we realized when looking at the back that they had been dyed," says Linda. "So the people doing the raffia restoration matched the colors and redyed them, and we put UV-protective museum-quality glass over them to preserve them."

Gillette's collections of frog figurines, pre-Columbian incense burners, and Jugtown pottery are back in place on the mantelpiece. "A lot of the little figurines he had actually cemented onto the fireplace. I don't know whether he thought his guests had light fingers or whether he was just worried they would break."

Gillette also designed special wooden locks, almost like puzzles, for each door and cabinet, including his liquor cabinet. "He would tell guests to help themselves, excuse himself for a moment, and go upstairs where he could see the bar from a mirror near his bedroom. He liked watching his guests, including Albert Einstein, try unsuccessfully to open the bar," says castle guide Kathy Burr. President Calvin Coolidge and actress Helen Hayes were guests here, though they lived quite simply in the

country estate, sleeping in bedrooms that were sparsely furnished.

The home is filled with William Gillette's book collection, his own writings and drawings, and even railroad models he designed as a child in Hartford. A portion of the top floor of the castle has been converted into a gallery for Gillette's paintings, a collection that numbers nearly one thousand. The basement is now an archive for scholars who wish to study his papers and scrapbooks.

And William Gillette, who spent so much of his life onstage, might be happy to know that thousands of people now tour his estate and its new visitor center and enjoy its woodland trails and river vistas. In his will he directed that his beloved Seventh Sister not become the possession of "some blithering saphead who has no conception of where he is, or with what surrounded."

Warren Kelley, the artistic director of the **River Rep Theatre Troupe,** picks up the story: "I think part of what happened was he tailored it to fit his particular charisma and his particular charm. . . . He became famous playing this role in a time before there were movies and television. Today you can become famous quickly. If you are Jerry Seinfeld and you do *Seinfeld* and it's a success, you can become famous within a year. The only way to be famous then was to be in the theater and play it night after night." Gillette played the role in Europe and across the United States until he was into his eighties.

During a recent strawhat summer season, Kelley's River Rep brought one of these plays to life at the Ivoryton Playhouse, just down the road from Gillette's home. Set in Victorian England, *Sherlock*

Holmes contains elements of Conan Doyle's "A Scandal in Bohemia" and "The Final Problem." Incriminating letters threaten a royal marriage, and Holmes must conquer his archenemy Professor Moriarity to save the heroine. "It's a series of traps that Sherlock has to deal with, and there are moments of real tension when you think he won't make it out of this one," says Kelley. "Of course he does because he is just one step quicker than anyone on stage, even the smartest person, who of course is Moriarity."

The play is great fun, and the set does it justice, designed as a revolving piece by Sesame Street art director Bob Phillips. Stephen Kunken, fresh from Broadway, has the look of Sherlock Holmes, though Kelley notes that playing Gillette's most famous role in the shadow of his own home was not intimidating for the lead actor.

"We don't remember what Gillette looks like and sounds like. Playing Henry Higgins in *My Fair Lady,* as I did, is tough because Rex Harrison's performance is indelible," Kelley says. "But in this case we don't have that memory of Gillette, so in a way it was freeing. Stephen could just take what's on the page and create such a convincing performance that I remember sitting there and thinking, *I bet this is what it was like.*"

Given the revivals that Gillette's home, his memorabilia, his parkland, and his plays have seen of late, we can all look around East Haddam and say *I bet this is what it was like.*

Boundless Playgrounds

Children enjoying a playground: Years have gone by, but the sight still reminds Amy Barzach of a lonely little girl in a wheelchair.

"I was with my three-year-old son Daniel and my four-month-old son Jonathan, who was healthy at the time," says Amy. "We saw this little girl in a wheelchair who so desperately wanted to play with the other children. And we thought, Shouldn't we have a playground where she could play, too?"

Amy could not have imagined that in the next few months that image would come to mean even more to her, as her baby was diagnosed with spinal muscular atrophy. Jonathan didn't live to see his first birthday.

"As we were struggling to deal with his illness, we remembered the little girl in the park," Amy recalls. "Shortly after he died we created a team of people to put together a playground. We wanted to build a playground where children of all abilities could play together as a memorial to Jonathan."

Amy and her husband raised three hundred thousand dollars and recruited twelve hundred volunteers to construct a fully accessible playground outside the West Hartford Jewish Community Center. Then she called in the experts to create a playground without boundaries—and who'd know better what kids would like than kids?

Matt Cavedon, who uses a wheelchair, knew the pain of sitting on the sidelines. "When I went to playgrounds, I couldn't play. I'd just sit and watch."

So Amy invited Matt to a party where kids were encouraged to dream and to design a place that would set their imaginations free. He invented a boat swing. "It creaks like an old boat and it just keeps moving," Matt says. "It rocks back and forth and sometimes you can just imagine that you're out on the ocean."

Amy understands that playgrounds are not just places where kids burn off energy. "It's how they learn to navigate the world," she says. "Playgrounds are where children learn about life. The idea of a playground is to give them a safe place where they can spread their wings and challenge themselves."

That playground became a blueprint for fully accessible playgrounds around the country. For one New Haven girl, Jonathan's Dream was a dream come true. She was only eight years old, but Hannah Kristan began a campaign to build a boundless playground in her own town.

"I had never been able to play in a park by myself because they weren't accessible," Hannah says. "I have a lot of friends in wheelchairs, and I thought we should be able to have a place to play with our friends who are able bodied. All kids need to play."

Hannah earned hundreds of dollars selling handmade jewelry and holding bake sales, then persuaded Easter Seals to take on the challenge of raising more than a quarter million dollars to build an accessible playground in New Haven's East Shore Park.

"I said it would be nice to bring the community together on a project like this," remembers Malcolm Gill, the director of the New Haven chapter of Easter Seals. "We had about one hundred people a day, union people working next to the vice president of a bank, putting nuts and bolts together."

On a tour with Hannah, she told us, "The swings over here are my favorite part, because they are swings for a person who can't sit up by themselves.

These swings have backs and they are more supportive for people. That's why I like them. I feel safe on them."

"I'm very proud of what Hannah has accomplished," beams Karen Scopino-Kristan, Hannah's mom. "She has taught me a lot about what people can do whether or not you have a disability. When I drive by this playground, I get chills, because I think of all the kids that are now going to have a place to play regardless of whether they're in a wheelchair or use crutches. They can have as much fun as other kids can have."

And that's the difference—in many playgrounds that meet the legal standards for accessibility, children with disabilities are still left out of the fun. Their wheelchairs or crutches can't navigate the flooring, and the equipment may not be designed for kids with physical challenges. Boundless playgrounds allow kids with disabilities to get into the center of the action.

When he was twelve years old, Matt Cavedon successfully lobbied the state legislature to budget one million dollars to help build boundless playgrounds across Connecticut. Some of that money will help build Devon's Place in Norwalk. Devon Jacoby is one of five thousand kids in lower Fairfield County who have special needs, including a more suitable place to play.

Devon's grandmother Doris wants to change that. Doris Jacoby says, "We have raised almost all of the $350,000 we need. We've gotten the money from some individuals and some local foundations and some from corporations."

And even some money from children in an inner-city school in Bridgeport. "This little kid comes up with a stained lunch bag, a little brown paper bag. I opened it and my husband and I burst into tears," says Doris. "It was filled with crumpled dollar bills and change, nothing bigger than a dollar bill. He says, 'There's ninety-eight dollars and eighty-five cents we collected.' Of all the money we've gotten, God love Paul Newman and his ten thousand included, nothing touched us more."

Devon's mother, Susan, says all kids need the opportunity to learn the social skills and gross and fine motor skills that are developed on the playground. Susan sees the playground as a place that will help change the world her daughter will grow up in: "I think that when people see other people in a wheelchair, they're hesitant to approach them or to get to know them. Maybe they're scared. . . . Building a playground like Devon's Place gives kids an opportunity to allay those fears and to see those children as people just like themselves."

Amy Barzach's nonprofit organization is helping communities from Rhode Island to California with technical assistance and fund-raising strategies to build more boundless playgrounds.

"So many of the parts of our boundless playground projects that were designed for kids with special needs are in fact the best places to play for everyone," Amy has discovered. "And I think that's a nice statement, because these are not just playgrounds for kids with disabilities, they're playgrounds for everybody."

ENJOYING THE GREAT OUTDOORS

KIDS JUST GOTTA HAVE FUN AT THE CHILDREN'S MUSEUM OF SOUTHEASTERN CONNECTICUT IN NIANTIC; A SACK RACE IN HARTFORD'S BUSHNELL PARK AT THE Y GAMES OF THE YMCA OF GREATER HARTFORD; KITE FESTIVAL AT HAMMONASSET BEACH STATE PARK IN MADISON; MAKING A SPLASH IN EAST NORWALK.

Painted Ponies

Nine-month-old Aaron Cholewa is celebrating Independence Day with his first ride on Hartford's Bushnell Park Carousel.

He's sitting on his mother Carol's lap in a bright chariot while his proud pop, Paul, shoots home video. The Newington parents were afraid the whirling carousel and the Wurlitzer band organ playing tunes from yesteryear, like "Let Me Call You Sweetheart," might alarm the baby. But Aaron loved it, bouncing merrily with the music.

The carousel was built in 1914 and installed in Hartford sixty years later. It is one of three surviving examples of the work of Russian immigrants and master carvers Solomon Stein and Harry Goldstein. The merry-go-round features thirty-six jumper horses and twelve standers with bulging eyes and flaring nostrils. Painted sea scenes embellish the carousel, along with delicately applied gold leaf. A twenty-four-sided wooden pavilion protects the ride. Fifty cents buys you a whirl into a nearly bygone era.

Between 1890 and 1930 there were as many as six thousand carousels in the United States. Today there are estimated to be only a few hundred antique

wooden carousels still operating across the country. A dozen merry-go-rounds dot Connecticut, according to Louise DeMars, the executive director of the New England Carousel Museum in Bristol and the Bushnell Park Carousel. Some are antiques, others modern reproductions made from resins and aluminum. The museum's Carousel Trail brochure identifies the locations of existing Connecticut carousels and marks the homes of those that are now extinct.

"Senior citizens love the carousel—they grew up with it as their entertainment form. Adults adore it. They remember their early days riding the carousel," Louise says. "It's the children today who don't have a lot of carousel experience. They're busy being bombarded with video games."

So the Carousel Museum formed an outreach program to educate kids about these disappearing wonders, like the Carousel at Lighthouse Point Park in New Haven. Assembled in 1916 in a Savin Rock

workshop, the wooden carousel is one of the largest anywhere, boasting seventy-two figures, including a camel, on a sixty-foot platform. For years a ride on the carousel was a highlight of a day at the beach. But time and all those damp bathing suits worn by riders took their toll on the horses, and the aging pavilion was damaged by sea air, storms, and hurricanes, forcing the city to board it up in 1977. Three years later the pavilion and carousel were under restoration, however, and an "Adopt A Horse" program provides funds to continue the upkeep.

In Bristol the New England Carousel Museum nurtures its own carving school, featuring artists like Juan Andreu from Spain, who has grown accustomed to working with an audience of admiring kids and adults. "It takes about three pieces of wood to make the head, then the body is one piece for the top and another piece for the bottom with a hollow center," Juan explains as a small crowd clusters around him. Juan restores antique animals and carves new ones, including some inspired by Connecticut's coastline—a manatee, a dolphin, and a sea otter.

From the smiling face of a baby on his first carousel ride to the giggling girls whirling on the merry-go-round that's been delighting children and adults at Lake Compounce Theme Park since 1911, it's clear Connecticut's carousels are treasures.

A Fair to Remember

Think Connecticut is just cities and suburbs? You'll think again after a visit to a Connecticut agricultural fair.

There are more than fifty fairs in the state each year, spread out from mid-July through mid-October, but the granddaddy of them all takes place in the "quiet corner" of the state, in Brooklyn.

The oldest agricultural fair in the USA—that's how the Brooklyn Fair proudly proclaims itself, going all the way back to 1809.

"Fairs started just as a reflection of society and what was happening," explains Sandy Eggers, the fair's vice president in charge of livestock and agriculture. "It started with the locals coming to compete against one another. They'd bring their horse, and they'd bring their cattle, and see who had the best animals."

And that's still a big part of the agricultural fair. In the show ring, it's a beauty contest for polled Herefords, their proud owners hungering for the blue ribbon or the trophies that gleam as sunlight filters into the barns.

Behind the scenes, as at any beauty pageant, the contestants are primping. One young man is scrubbing a huge pink pig, while nine-year-old Leah Gankofskie and twelve-year-old Aubrey Desjarlais are wielding hand shears, getting Lilly, a registered Hampshire sheep, ready to show. Lilly was raised by the girls from the time she was born. "We fed her a bottle every morning," says Aubrey.

While the pride of Plum Gully Farm and the other entrants entertain visitors in their dressing rooms (also known as stalls by some), all that trimmed fleece isn't going to waste. Shelby Grant plans to finish a scarf. "I spun it and then I knit this,

and I need more to make a fringe." That scarf may be entered in the crafts competition and displayed alongside beribboned giant dahlias and prizewinning apples, peaches, pumpkins, and pies.

"It means an awful lot for a child to win one of those ribbons," Sandy explains, "because it's a reflection of a whole year's worth of work. They don't just take something out of their backyard and bring it in. They've worked with these animals or they've grown the produce that they're showing or made the crafts, and it means a lot because it's a part of them."

The fair is not just about kids, though. James Palmer is showing Dave and Eddy, the pair of shorthorn oxen he rescued and now uses for logging.

"When I first got them you could count ribs up to about here," James says as he strokes Eddy. "The guy who owned them didn't feed them very well, so that's how the Humane Society ended up with them, before I took them home."

Children and adults compete in the English and Western riding classes in the horse show, and for one day a year, the Brooklyn Fairgrounds offers the only harness racing in Connecticut. Russell Lawson's Standardbred stallion, Buzz B King, is feeling his oats as he whinnies at the other horses passing by his pen.

"It's one place where you can go out and have a good time and not worry about winning or losing,

because the purses aren't high enough to worry about it much," Russell says with a grin as he hitches up his sulky to the stallion.

The midway attractions, rides, and concessions help pay for the heart of the fair: the agricultural competition. According to historian Bob Brockett, "The major reason for having a fair was to transfer information between the farmers so that they could improve their production. This is still a major part of most of the fairs. Several of them give over twenty thousand dollars in premium money for the best animals, the best produce, or the best work from the kitchen."

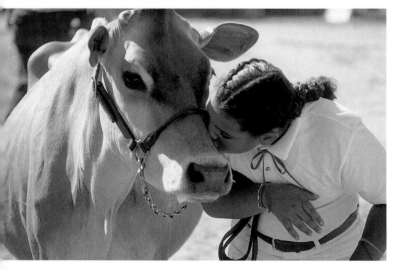

Bob should know. One summer he visited each of Connecticut's fifty-four agricultural fairs.

Much of what you see at the agricultural fairs celebrates Connecticut's farm heritage, but in truth the agricultural economy is changing much like the rest of our economy, and the fairs are an opportunity for farmers to connect with consumers, says Sandy Eggers. "They have to see what the people are looking for and deliver it to them."

That may mean attracting tourists to their operations with demonstrations of chain-saw sculpting or shearing pricey fleece from alpacas. "Right now a lot of what's happening in state agriculture is forestry, and greenhouse work. Hydroponics greenhouses are a big deal, and it's important that people have a chance to see these things and know what's happening around them," she continues. "As society has become more removed from their agricultural roots, a lot of these families just aren't aware of it. This is a great opportunity for them to come in here and see a little bit of things so that they realize that milk doesn't come from a jar, it comes from a cow."

Sandy adds that the spectacle of the agricultural fairs says something about the vitality of agriculture in Connecticut. "Agriculture is not dead at all; it's changed. Everything evolves, and the fairs just evolve along with them."

TOP ROW: TRACTORS AND KIDDIE RIDES AT THE BROOKLYN FAIR. MIDDLE ROW: A BOY AND HIS CALF AT THE CHESTER FAIR; A GIRL AND HER ROOSTER AT THE BROOKLYN FAIR. BOTTOM ROW: AT THE CHESTER FAIR, OXEN WAIT TO PULL THEIR WEIGHT, AWARD-WINNING PICKLED PRODUCE IS DISPLAYED PROUDLY AGAINST A FIELD OF FLOWERS, AND A TEEN TRIMS HER SHEEP IN PREPARATION FOR A SHOWMANSHIP CLASS. FACING PAGE: TWO CHILDREN PREPARE TO SHOW THEIR ANIMALS AT THE BROOKLYN FAIR.

Museums of Trucks and Time

What to do on a rainy summer's day in Connecticut? Two unique museums are set up to engross both you and the young ones in two very different facets of our Yankee heritage.

In Middlebury a museum celebrates the transportation industry with galleries full of gleamingly restored big rigs—Macks, Studebakers, Dodge and Diamond vehicles—along with interactive children's exhibits, a reading room, special events, and even a "Truck of the Month."

It's called the **Golden Age of Trucking Museum,** but it might as well be called the museum of love, because this *is* a love story—about a man's passion for trucks, his love for a woman and their kids, and how his family fulfilled his dream after he was gone.

The airplane-hangar–sized museum was the brainchild of Dick Guerrera, who had loved trucks since he was a boy and grew up to run a successful trucking business. Along the way he also fell in love with Fran, then a thirty-year-old woman with five

small children. For their honeymoon—well, you guessed it.

"We flew to California and we drove a Peterbilt back because he had to have a Peterbilt," Fran smiles as she remembers. "Because no one else had one on the East Coast."

Dick and Fran had one more child together, and they all grew to embrace his first love, spending family vacations on trips that always seemed to include a stop at a junkyard. "He would always say, 'It'll just be a minute,' and we knew that was trouble," says his daughter Kathi Jones, with a gleam in her eye. "We would be there for a few hours. Now when I look back on it, how lucky we were—it was wonderful."

When his kids were mostly raised and his transport business was doing well, Dick began indulging his passion for vintage vehicles. Fran says he just couldn't pass by a tired old workhorse. "He would start seeing older trucks on the side of the road in disarray and that bothered him terribly! He just couldn't stand that. So he bought one that he had owned once and sold to someone else and then saw in disrepair on the side of the road. He bought it back and restored it, and that was the beginning."

Eventually Dick's collection grew to more than sixty rigs, mostly from the 1950s through the 1970s according to his pal and fellow "truck nut" Bob Manchester. "To us, the people who like diesel engines, the sound and the mystique and the power of them, the 1950s were truly the start of the golden age of trucking."

But Dick would not live to see the museum he had long imagined. Gravely ill with colon cancer, he did make it to one milestone. "It was Father's Day, and we all gathered here on the property he had purchased for the museum, and we brought him here in the ambulance," Fran says warmly. "We took him out of the ambulance and my son John took the shovel and we broke ground for his museum."

Not long after, Dick Guerrera passed away, and Fran decided on a fitting final tribute. "Jokingly he would say, 'When I die I want you to prop me up in one of the trucks.' We did the next best thing. We carried him to his resting place in the big orange truck you see over there."

And then his family built his museum. "It was my dad's dream," Kathi says, "so we just followed through on it because that's what he wanted. And because *he* wanted it, *we* wanted it."

Fran swears Dick's spirit permeates the place. "I buried Dick on our thirtieth wedding anniversary," she says. "We were together thirty years and I'll tell you, it was quite a ride. It really was."

Remember the days before Waterbury's Brass Mill Center mall, when the site at the junction of Routes 8 and 84 was jammed with crumbling remnants of the Brass City's biggest industries? Sixty-five of those buildings were torn down, but one was saved. Once the executive offices of Scoville Manufacturing, it's now the **Timexpo Museum,** recalling the era when Waterbury's brass and clock-making industries merged and made Connecticut the leading clock-making region in the country.

Museum curator Carl Rosa grew up here and remembers those old factories. "Timex is a descendant of those companies, and the last American watch company headquartered in the U.S. We are tenants in a historic building, and we wanted to preserve its integrity while turning it into a top-flight museum." Timex's lab, accounting, and corporate offices are still in Middlebury.

The exhibit emphasizes the rich horological tradition of the Naugatuck Valley, where in the 1880s clockmakers, using brass inner workings, produced some of the most elaborate and now collectible clocks ever made. There are mantel and alarm clocks, hanging and grandfather clocks, boudoir and novelty clocks, calendar and carriage clocks. Carl searched far and wide, buying up the clocks made by Timex's ancestor, the Waterbury Clock Company.

Once a week or so you'll find Arthur Torrence here, repairing those fine old clocks. Now retired and a volunteer at the museum, Arthur loves the painstaking work and talking to visitors. "It's always been my hobby," he says. "I've been working on

clocks since I was a kid. Most of them come in here in pretty bad condition." Before the brass mills turned out the makings for metal inner workings of clocks, they were made from wood. "Actually, they kept time pretty well," Arthur says. There are about thirteen hundred clocks in the collection. So far Arthur and other volunteers have refurbished about 40 percent of them.

"We're about as much a part of Waterbury's history as you can get and about as much a part of industrial history as you can get in the last two hundred years," says Louis Galie, the president of Timexpo. Interactive exhibits at the museum allow kids to design their own watches from cardboard, while their grandparents reminisce about the "torture tests" that John Cameron Swayze put Timex watches through—the ones that "take a licking and keep on ticking."

If you wonder about the colossal statue outside, it's a replica of those created in places like Polynesia and Easter Island. Why is it here? Timex owners supported the explorations of Norwegian Thor Heyerdahl. In 1947 he traveled five thousand miles in a woven reed raft called *Kon Tiki* to try to prove that ancient man moved from one continent to the next using the ocean's currents as highways. One

floor of the museum is dedicated to Heyerdahl's controversial theories.

From the travels of early man, to the history of Connecticut's manufacturing heyday, to the timepieces of tomorrow (watches that download information from your computer or contain, store, and play two hours of your favorite music)—you'll find it all at the Timexpo Museum, a place that keeps on ticking through all the showers a summer in Connecticut might bring.

Amaizing Mazes

How would you like to get lost in four acres of Corn-ecticut? Lots of people do, because navigating mazes created in living cornfields is, you might say, a growing trend in the state. The Connecticut aMaizeing Maze on the **Eddinger Farm** in Middletown has a new theme each year, with forage corn, the kind fed to animals, planted in elaborate designs, and two miles of intertwining winding paths. Families try to solve the three-dimensional interactive puzzle in a game that combines education, agriculture, and, when seen from the air, a unique form of art. Special events include hayrides and Moonlight in the Maze in midsummer.

Lyman Orchards in Middletown operates a maze designed with the help of a computer. When seen from above, one year's maze resembled their famous high-top apple pie. The farm boasts that its maze has eighty-five decision points and several lookout bridges to get a better look at, well, all that corn. A portion of the proceeds benefits the American Cancer Society.

One year **Plasko's Farm** in Trumbull chose a patriotic theme, an eagle surrounded by stars, while in South Windsor the **Foster Family Farm** featured a medieval fantasy for visitors with two full-sized corn mazes visited by lords and ladies, one patterned after a dragon and another after a wizard. There's a mini maze for beginners and the little ones, too. And in Brookfield **Larson's Farm Market** offers a seven-acre underwater adventure maze, with a puzzle to solve as you wend your way through the trails. While you're there, pick up some sweet corn.

Corn maze openings are extremely weather dependent. Some open by mid-July, while others open later. It's a good idea to call ahead before setting out on a family adventure.

History Alive

Twenty years ago, not long after I had moved to Connecticut, my sister Suzanne flew in from Los Angeles to visit me at my New Haven apartment. "What would like to see while you're here?" I asked. "Just take me to see something old," she said. "I miss that in LA."

So we strolled around the Yale campus, taking in buildings that date back to 1750 and peeking inside the three churches on the green—one Gothic, one Federalist, one Georgian. I began to see my new home through Suzanne's eyes, not as a city that time had worn, but as a place where history was alive in modern times, with roots that tie us to our nation's founding.

You, too, can see history come alive all summer long in Connecticut. Dedicated reenactors are at work here re-creating history with all its sounds and tastes and smells. Some, like Kevin Johnson, spend the precious hours of summer poring over archives, notes, and documents to bring their characters to life. They may be welders, or dentists, or insurance agents in this century, but in their souls, they are the reborn embodiments of the men and women who helped form this great nation.

Of course, the story of Connecticut is older than the history of our country, and the Mashantucket Pequot Museum and Research Center's Schemitzun, a Native American display of dance and rodeo, shows us what life was like here before Connecticut was even a British colony. Village greens, ancient burial grounds, forts from the Revolutionary War, Mark Twain's homestead, and whaling villages like Stonington are all reminders of the Connecticut that came before us. Annual events like the blessing of the fishing fleet are touchstones reminding us that the past and present are intertwined.

Something Old, Something New . . . Something New-Gate

A cannon fires, a fife and drum corps plays, a colonial regiment marches by.

Women in colonial garb are cooking over an open fire beside row upon row of simple white linen tents with military cots inside. When this is your idea of camping with friends, and when the love of your life is also in love with early American history, what better way to begin a marriage than among these companions with an eighteenth-century-style wedding?

"Dearly beloved, we are gathered here in the sight of God," intones Justice of the Peace Evan Wollacott to family, friends—and gathered tourists, too. After all, this wedding is taking place at one of Connecticut's most historic sites, the Old New-Gate Prison

and Copper Mine. The bride and groom, Tina Louise Chassee and Peter Johnson, are reenactors with Ye Olde Lebanon Town Militia, an organization that traces its roots back to the Revolutionary War.

So they recited vows taken from the pages of history. Tina repeats after the minister: "With this ring I thee wed, with my body I thee worship."

After the ceremony Peter says he doesn't mind having strangers watching. "We're used to the public being around, so that doesn't bother us in the least. It's a thrill to be able to say you had a thousand people at your wedding."

Their wedding finery was fashioned with authentic style. In an age before brides wore white, Tina's green-and-ecru gown, known as a "sack back Polonaise," would have been the height of elegance, although on a steaming summer's day it was a little uncomfortable.

"It's a hair hotter than what a modern bride would wear because I have so many layers," she admits. "One thing I have that a modern bride doesn't have is a set of stays underneath."

The Johnsons' wedding (which was real) was the highlight of a weekend when the Lebanon Militia and Fifth Connecticut Regiment breathed life into history at a place that began as a copper mine in 1701. But when the British Crown issued a command that all raw materials be shipped to England for processing, the mine began to lose money.

"So in 1773 the colonial government bought the place, and their idea was to use convicts as miners," according to Chris Riley, New-Gate's manager. A cellblock was built on the site and became our first federal prison, housing Tories loyal to the throne. "Only trouble is, the convicts kept digging escape tunnels and braining the guards. It's very hard to supervise convicts in the dark anyway."

Tom Angels, a member of the Fifth Connecticut Regiment, is encamped for the weekend and per-forming in the elaborate skits. "The public is so receptive to history live. It means so much more to children and adults than out of the book, because they get the smells, the tastes, the sounds, and the visuals of what period life was like back then."

Entire families are involved in the reenact-ment—kids, grandkids, and even great-grand-children. Peter Eldridge, who is finely turned out, is holding his great-granddaughter Savannah, also wearing colonial garb. "We love talking to the pub-lic," Peter says. "That's our major function, to talk to the visitors."

While the reenactors are having fun, Ruth Daly notes that their hobby means they are committed to preserving and sharing our history. "If you don't know your history, you are doomed to repeat it. There's a lot of basic tenets that our country was founded on, and people have a tendency to forget what those are."

Visitors like Merle Pederson from Richmond, Virginia, do get the message. "Somebody has to make history palatable enough so people will pay attention. There's too much history lost."

Meanwhile the bride and groom are cutting their wedding cake with a Revolutionary-era sword. Sav-ing a slice of history: For some it's a passion and a pleasure.

CONNECTICUT CLASSICS

CLOCKWISE FROM TOP LEFT: FINE STONEWORK AT THE WHITFIELD HOUSE IN GUILFORD; COLORFUL GINGERBREAD IN WOODSTOCK; RUSTIC TONES IN DURHAM; AN ELEGANT WHITE COLONIAL IN ESSEX; WEATHERED WOOD ADDS CHARACTER TO A COVERED BRIDGE IN EAST HADDAM.

Ferry Land

In Rocky Hill, Chester, and Bridgeport, three ferries with a long history of plying the local waters keep Connecticut connected.

As the nation's oldest continuously operating ferry, the **Rocky Hill–Glastonbury ferry** has been here almost as long as there have been people in Connecticut. Local families operated the service as early as 1655. By the time the state took over, the service had been in place nearly three hundred years!

"They represent the basic ferryboats that were used all through time, except for poles and horses on treadmills," says Jim Grant, the lead captain of his fleet of two. "But the tug and barge system they use in Rocky Hill is a distinctive way of ferrying." The crossing takes only four minutes, and the barge can carry three or four cars.

Downriver a ferry has connected the scenic towns of **Chester and Hadlyme** since 1769. During its four-minute trip the *Selden-3* hauls up to nine cars, as well as passengers arriving on bikes or on foot. It has been featured in everything from a Billy Joel video to a Troy Donahue movie.

The double-ended ferryboat is the delight of commuters and sightseers, too. "I think a lot of people like to use the ferryboats to get away from the traffic," Jim says. "There is a wait, but it actually makes you stop and reflect and soak in the scenery. It brings you back to nature—the birds chirping, the deer off in the distance in the morning—and it's really a beautiful sight."

Some passengers are tourists headed for Gillette Castle; others are daily commuters. Donna Gohn of Hadlyme looks forward to the months the ferry is

operating. "It's a nice way to go anywhere, start your trip, shopping, or go to work or whatever." Ann Lightfoot hops the ferry when she's picking up her kids—"anytime I have to get to the other side of the river. It's more picturesque."

Tidal changes mean you have stay on your toes while at the helm. No problem for Captain John F. Kennedy, a former tugboat captain in New York Harbor. Boating must be in his blood—his father was assigned to the U.S. Coast Guard barque *Eagle* when he met the captain's namesake. "Some people, this is their very first boat ride here, and they think the world of it. When I was five years old, my mother was taking me for a ride and I can remember right about here looking at that dock over there and thinking, This ride is just too short."

Diane Darcy is the first mate, because, she says, "I enjoy the public. I have a good time talking to people from all over the world." People like Serra Simbeck, who is visiting from San Antonio, Texas, and says: "This is absolutely the most beautiful part of the United States as far as I'm concerned."

The river ferries are dwarfed by their three-hundred-foot-long cousins in Long Island Sound, but the **Bridgeport and Port Jefferson Steamboat Company** also has a proud history. It was founded in 1883 by the legendary P. T. Barnum.

"The original concept of the ferry was to link the agricultural products of Long Island with some of the city services—banking, dentistry, and so forth—available here in Bridgeport," according to Fred Hall, the general manager. Today the fleet of three carries passengers who come for Bridgeport's arena, baseball field, and theaters, as well as passengers headed for boutiquing and waterfront dining in Port Jefferson, Long Island.

While the state's small historic ferries close down for the winter and come back in spring, the Port Jeff–Bridgeport service runs year-round no matter what the weather. In fact, this ferry can take pretty much whatever Long Island Sound can dish out. Captain Edward O'Neill says of his ship: "She spans out over the seas. We have good speed, we can get around whatever we want, slow down, good maneuverability, visibility, everything."

With the trip of seventeen nautical miles taking just over an hour, it's an alternative to highway traffic. The boats can carry a thousand passengers and up to 120 cars. Last year the fleet carried 425,000 cars, more than ten times the number it transported just a few years ago. As passenger Randy Howie from Ridgefield says, "It's just a nice thing to do."

This Thing Called Freedom

All summer long, while most people are heading for the beach or a shady picnic ground, Kevin Johnson is headed for the Connecticut State Library and Museum of Connecticut History.

Summer is when Kevin researches the characters he plays in his one-man shows about African Americans in the Revolutionary and Civil Wars.

"I'm no longer bound, no more chains holding me, and my soul is resting and it's such a blessing, to praise the Lord, hallelujah! I'm free!" Shouting out

those words, this Civil War soldier seems to have stepped out of time and into the auditorium of the Orchard Hill School in South Windsor.

"Freedom! I said it sounds good and it sounds nice! Got to be free! Greetings to all of you. My name is Private William Riley Salisbury Webb and I'm with the Twenty-ninth Connecticut Volunteers and I fought in the Civil War," the soldier tells his spellbound audience.

Kevin Johnson works in the History and Genealogy Unit at the Connecticut State Library. Always a history buff, Kevin's interest in Connecticut's African-American soldiers in the Civil War began in 1997 when he was asked to pose for a photograph at the Bushnell Arch commemorating the state's Freedom Trail, wearing a borrowed Civil War uniform. From there he uncovered the life of a real man, in the records and documents at the state library.

"We scrolled down the enlistment papers. We wanted to find a gentleman from Hartford. Private Webb was where my finger stopped, and that was it," says Kevin. "My curiosity led me to want to know a lot more about who this guy was."

Kevin searched through the library's archives, finding census data, a record of Webb's mother's marriage, evidence that Webb was incarcerated for a time in Wethersfield, and then his army enlistment papers. Webb joined the Twenty-ninth, one of two all-black regiments from Connecticut made up of freemen as well as runaway slaves from the South.

selves to their white and sometimes skeptical commanding officers. Abolitionist Frederick Douglass saw this as a watershed.

"Douglass said, once the black man gets upon his person the brass letters *U.S.* and an eagle on his button and a musket on his shoulder and bullets in his pocket, there is no power on earth that can deny that the black man has earned the right to be a citizen in the United States," Kevin nearly shouts with pride.

It was a long road for Kevin Johnson from his first job to teaching about the Civil War in schools, churches, and museums. Indeed, it was almost literally a road, since he started out as a toll taker on the Merritt Parkway. When the tollbooths closed, the state sent him to the library on a job interview. And as Kevin likes to say, "The rest is history!"

"What Kevin is doing is a wonderful way to interest young people in why history and archives are important," says Kendall Wiggin, the state librarian. "It shows how you can learn about the life of a simple soldier. He wasn't the general, he wasn't the leader, but you can take a soldier's life and see how it evolved."

Bobby Otaluka was impressed by Kevin's performance. "I thought it was very good because of the way he knew so much about the person that he was doing."

"This is what students are going to remember about their fifth-grade experience when they become adults. They're not going to remember page 378 in the social studies book," says Jennifer Oliver, their social studies teacher.

In the final months of the war, William Webb was sent home after sustaining an injury that would eventually blind him, but the Twenty-ninth regiment soldiered on. Recently one of its musket rifles was donated to the library's museum.

Kevin chokes up as he holds it in his hands and exclaims, "This was held by one of our guys that was fighting for freedom. That I sit here, that I live every day—well, if it wasn't for these guys willing to give their lives to this thing called freedom, I wouldn't be talking with you right now."

"They were some good men that were going to prove to be great soldiers, once given the opportunity to fight," Kevin tells the children in his audience.

Blacks were not allowed to enlist until more than a year into the Civil War. They had to prove them-

HISTORICAL MUSTERS AND REENACTMENTS

CLOCKWISE FROM TOP LEFT: A FIFER IN THE
FIFES AND DRUMS OF YORK TOWN AT THE
DEEP RIVER ANCIENT MUSTER; SOLDIERS MAN
THE CANNON AT FORT NATHAN HALE IN NEW
HAVEN; ANCIENT MARINERS DRUM LINE AT
THE DEEP RIVER ANCIENT MUSTER; CIVIL WAR
FINERY (RIGHT) AND REENACTMENT (LEFT) AT
HAMMONASSET STATE BEACH, MADISON.

A Brave Revenge

If thirty-seven other states can stage outdoor historical dramas each summer, then why not Connecticut, where much of our nation's history began?

That's what John Basinger, a retired theater professor, and Dave Holdridge, a retired history professor, colleagues at Three Rivers Community College in Norwich, decided. After all, Norwich is the birthplace of one of the most famous figures in early American history, Benedict Arnold, who went from hero to traitor, returning to his beloved New London with the British army to burn the city and assault Groton Heights in 1781.

"Dave had the idea for the two hundredth anniversary of the invasion in 1981," says John, "but it took another twenty years to bring it to fruition."

But isn't Benedict Arnold a reviled character in American history? "Benedict Arnold is an enormously complex person and so easy to love as you

are doing the research on him," according to John. "If they had SAT scores in those days, and if they had all-American athletes, he would have been at the absolute top at everything. Unquestionably the guy was just smarter than anybody else around him, but that may have been his undoing in a sense. When you are really special, just by breathing you make enemies, and it seems that's what happened."

In midsummer 2003 the pair finally saw their idea come to life in a grand spectacle of history, patriotism, and community. Their cast of dozens performed five shows on an outdoor stage constructed at Washington Park in Groton and drew thousands to see the drama that had long ago unfolded in their backyard.

"It's the blood-soaked-soil syndrome," John says, chuckling. "These plays work best where you can actually see the roots of the history. It's a site-specific kind of thing. Then the people get behind it. For example, Averys died in the siege in 1781 and we have Averys in the cast who are direct lineal descendants of these people, so it's actually quite thrilling."

The cast is an amalgam of professional (Equity) actors, local community theater performers, historical reenactors, and area residents with no acting experience who just wanted to be part of re-creating history. One even donated her horse to play Arnold's glorious steed.

Brian Jennings, a professional actor from Chester who teaches at the Greater Hartford Academy of the Arts, plays Brigadier General Benedict Arnold. It's clear he relishes the role. "I am not an evil-looking guy, so I never really get cast as bad guys. I am always someone who is rather nice and ineffectual, so this is a great deal of fun."

In May the cast started lessons in singing, dancing, and fight technique. "Fight captain" Ashley

Burgess learned her technique from David Chandler, a fight choreographer at the O'Neill National Theater Institute in Waterford. Most of the "colonists" wielding axes and rifles and "soldiers" armed with muskets, bayonets, and swords are complete amateurs.

"We do a lot of trust exercises," explains Ashley. "It's a lot about eye contact, which is most important. It's really about accuracy and not speed."

For some, learning the dancing was nearly as hard. Fortunately they had Marc Casslar from Bloomfield teaching them. An environmental consultant by day, Marc is an expert in eighteenth-, nineteenth-, and early-twentieth-century dances.

"Nineteen years ago I saw a couple performing late nineteenth-century dances and I was hooked, although I can't tell you why," he says, shaking his head. He even started his own vintage dance ensemble. "They have traveled and performed all over the U.S., even in Japan three times."

John Basinger's friend of twenty years, Neely Bruce, composed the music, writing much that's original and weaving in some traditional tunes.

"The song 'Columbia' ends the show, which I wish I had written although I did do the arrangement of it. It's a very, very powerful tune, an anonymous tune with a text by Timothy Dwight. It was written during the Revolution, and he was imagining the glorious future of America rising out of the confusion and destruction of the war that was going on around him when he wrote this."

On each night of its premiere run, *Benedict Arnold: A Brave Revenge* attracted enthusiastic crowds who arrived early with lawn chairs and picnic baskets and lots of kids in tow. The five-day run also doubled the number of history buffs who visited nearby Fort Griswold to see where the drama really took place.

"This is one of the most worthwhile projects I have ever been involved in in my life," composer Neely Bruce declares. "There are so many things I believe in about this. The theater is very powerful. I like doing work that's historically grounded and culturally aware. And I like being involved in projects that build community, which this has done magnificently!"

Deep History

The human fascination with submarines runs deep. From the earliest attempt to build a sub—David Bushnell's *Turtle* in 1776; to the first modern-day submarine, delivered by John Holland to the U.S. Navy in 1900; to today's nuclear-powered submarine fleet, we have marveled that people can live and wage war beneath the ocean. Since 1916 every submariner has learned these skills at Naval Submarine Base New London in Groton. So it makes sense that's where the Submarine Force Museum and Library is located, and where the fleet's most famous retired boat, the USS *Nautilus*, is docked.

A new permanent exhibit called the Medal of Honor Gallery honors the eight submariners who have been awarded the medal, including one hero from Connecticut—Putnam's Henry Breault, who was honored almost eighty years ago. A summer visit here makes a perfect way to spend a day near the cool sea air while engaging your mind as well.

The U.S. Navy has documented sub history in its entirety in this collection, which includes more than eighteen thousand artifacts, twenty thousand documents, and thirty thousand photos. You'll see John Holland's bill to the navy for his submarine ($150,000) as well as information detailing the development of World War II's diesel-powered subs.

During the Cold War era, submarine warfare changed forever. Fifty years ago Admiral Hyman Rickover commissioned the first nuclear powered submarine, the *Nautilus,* which is now a decommissioned, national landmark docked on the Thames River and available to tour.

"By putting nuclear power plants into the subs, we were able to make them truly submersible. They were no longer dependent on the atmosphere at all," says the museum's director, Lieutenant Commander Ben Howard. "It gave us higher speeds that we could operate at for indefinite periods of time. It allowed us to put subs out to sea with nuclear missiles on them and keep them continuously submerged and make them impossible to find."

The end of the Cold War has seen a rise in regional conflicts, and the sub force has responded. And as long as there are submarines, Sub Base Commander Ray Lincoln says New London will be the submarine capital of the world. "We have a deep-rooted sense that this is our home because our soul is here."

Bravery and Bagpipes

The drone of bagpipes: Since September 11 their sound is synonymous with sorrow, especially for those in the brotherhood of police and firefighters, like veteran Bloomfield police officer Ken Barber.

"When you hear the pipes, at least for me, I have a memory and I have a connection to all the officers who have passed and all those that will go in the future," Ken says. "Unfortunately, there will be some in the future. So we have that link. When I'm playing, it's not me; I'm invoking that spirit."

That spirit is so important to Ken that he spends hours each week drilling members of the Manchester Regional Police and Fire Pipe Band. The band marches in Memorial Day parades like the one in

Tolland. "When we go by reviewing stands in parades, the hairs on the back of my neck stand up," admits Manchester police detective Russ Wood, who marches with his daughter MacKinnon, a tenor drum player.

"The tenor drum is the drum that does most of the flourishing. It's the showy type of instrument, I guess you could say. We do all the spinning. When you see the sticks flying, it's usually us," MacKinnon explains.

Some of the pipers feel a special connection with their heritage, like music teacher Christine Corcoran, one of several women members. "I was very involved with Celtic music as a child. I did Irish step dancing forever, accordion lessons like a good Irish girl did. My maiden name was O'Neill."

Pipe bands have long been associated with police and firefighters, thanks to the large influx of Scottish and Irish immigrants into the United States in the late 1800s; many found jobs in newly formed urban departments. But this band brings together people from all over—kids in middle and high school, teachers, a surgeon, a lawyer, cops, and firefighters like Hal Grout. "I've found that pipes either make you want to cry or make you fight. I guess that's why they're great in war and they're good at funerals," he says with a laugh.

The Highland pipes are made up of three drones, a bass and two tenors, which provide the constant pitch in the background that sounds like bees buzzing. The blowpipe fills the bag with air, and squeezing at the same time with your arm maintains the steady pressure to keep the tones constant. Then there's the chanter, the part the musician fingers to produce the music.

"Most musicians playing other instruments would think it's only a one-octave instrument," says Russ. "So it should be easy, but the speed with which it has to be done and the timing make it a difficult instrument to play."

"People think you must have great lungs and great blowing capability," Hal adds. "If your bagpipes are set up properly, there's a little effort involved—but not as much as one would think."

Weekly rehearsals find the band in T-shirts and

jeans, but parades and competitions call for regalia based on the uniforms of the Scottish regiments that go back to the 1700s, including a kilt in the tartan known as the Hunting Stewart and a horsehair sporran—once used as a purse.

The band is now one of the biggest in the Northeast, with fifty-seven uniformed and active members, but their goal is to double in size. If you're interested, you can drop by one of their practices on Tuesday nights at the old soap factory on Hilliard Street in Manchester.

The Manchester Regional Police and Fire Pipe Band has two sacred trusts: keeping alive the heritage of Irish and Scottish immigrants, and honoring and supporting police and firefighters. Members fulfill both, in a spirit of hope for Connecticut's future.

Amazing Airmen

A rainy summer's day at the New England Air Museum in Windsor Locks is a chance to view the aircraft of all sorts that led to modern-day aviation.

One exhibit honors the Tuskegee Airmen, the World War II pilots who broke the barriers of color to soar with eagles. A handful of the airmen still live in the area.

"I was a little fella walking down Wooster Street in Hartford, so small I was holding my dad's hand." It was seventy-five years ago, but Connie Nappier remembers the day he knew he would become a pilot. "I heard a loud noise so I grabbed his hand," recalls Connie, his eyes narrowing. "I said, 'What's that?' He pointed and said, 'See that? That's an airplane.' I think right then I knew I wanted to fly." But Connie was in for a surprise. "It never occurred to me that I would have any difficulty because my complexion was a bit darker."

Connie saw his chance in World War II, when the segregated armed services yielded to pressure from civil rights groups. An old newsreel tells the story: "In July of 1941 five young Negroes made aviation history in Tuskegee, Alabama. These five men were the first of their race to graduate under the Army Air Forces' newly organized plan for training Negro pilots."

Lemuel Rodney Custis, the first black policeman in Hartford, was in that first class, and he inspired Connie. "I went down to apply for the exam and that's when the fight started," he says.

It would be a mighty struggle. George Hardy, now a retired lieutenant colonel, would become one of the youngest pilots sent overseas with the Ninety-ninth Fighter Squadron, made up of those first African-American airmen. "When you finally graduated and they gave you your wings, that was just a memorable moment you never forgot," George says.

George's squadron was commanded by the legendary Benjamin O. Davis Jr., who later became the first black general in the air force. George Hardy flew twenty-one combat missions escorting bombers from northern Italy into Germany. "It wasn't a matter of we're going to prove something to someone else," George explains. "It was that we're going to prove to *ourselves* that we can fly and we're going to prove as a group that we can do as well as anyone else."

And they did. The fighter unit had a perfect record, never losing a bomber to enemy fighters. The Tuskegee Airmen distinguished themselves, destroying or damaging 409 German aircraft and more than 950 units of ground transportation. They even sank a destroyer. But when he returned home to the United States, George found some things hadn't changed. "The army at that time had rules that blacks and whites could not sleep together, eat together, or be together," he recalls ruefully.

CONNIE NAPPIER   LEMUEL RODNEY CUSTIS   GEORGE HARDY

Even after the military was integrated in 1948, George encountered racism, this time during the Korean War with his squadron commander. "He told me to get down out of the airplane and he replaced me with a major who was white," he remembers. That decision may have saved George's life. "It so happened that that airplane was the first B-29 shot down over Korea."

As a trained aviation mechanic when he joined the service, James Sheppard was in great demand during World War II, keeping the fighters flying from Italy. "I'd like people to realize we were no different, absolutely no different, than the white fighter groups two miles up the road; that given the chance to train and perform our units, the black units, performed just as well."

When the army decided it had enough black aviators, Connie Nappier's dream to become a pilot was stalled. So he wrote to President Roosevelt. "I laid the whole thing out that I had met all the qualifications and that I should have an opportunity to learn to fly," he says, still smoldering all these decades later.

He made it into the air corps. But before Connie finished his training came an incident that would change his life and change the U.S. military. In April 1945, while Connie was stationed at Freeman Field in Indiana, black aviators were refused service in the officers' club. Later, a military tribunal ordered the men to sign a statement saying they understood why they could not use the club. When they refused to sign, they were locked up. They had disobeyed a direct order in a time of war, and they knew the penalty could be death.

"We woke up one morning and found that President Roosevelt had passed away, and we were informed that our new president was Harry S. Truman, who was from Missouri, which meant he was a southerner. We were pretty convinced that we would be shot," he states.

But Truman set them free, and Connie Nappier finally earned his wings. "I'll always remember that day when I got her off the ground. I looked around and saw the earth below me, and it was like I was one of the angels or something," he says.

Though the war ended before he ever flew a combat mission, Connie doesn't regret a moment of his fight to fly. "I've soared like an eagle; I've dived like a hawk. I've played tag with the clouds. I've reached out and touched the face of God."

Those memories are now part of a tribute to the Tuskegee Airmen at the New England Air Museum. "These people are heroes. They put up with things that other people who risked their lives equally just didn't have to put up with," says museum director Michael Speciale. "We need to tell the story, we need to look back, we need to understand that things weren't always necessarily the way they should have been in the United States. I think that helps make us a better place now."

"This is *my* country—I don't care what anyone says," Connie declares. "This is my country and I will do my part. Even now I would go right back at it."

The Tuskegee Airmen have at long last been honored for their patriotism and valor. It's been a long flight to freedom.

Schemitzun

Schemitzun is the largest showcase of Native American culture on the East Coast. Each August, the Mashantucket Pequots' Festival of Green Corn and Dance attracts the finest Native American dancers, who compete for hundreds of thousands of dollars in prizes. The festival's roots are found in early harvest celebrations: When the first ears of corn ripened in summer, Native Americans gathered for games, dancing, and prayer. Music is a big part of today's festival. Drum groups perform, and singing includes traditional songs in Native languages as well as modern-day songs in English. The Buck-a-Rama features bull riding and rodeo events. The festival even offers Native American arts and crafts and foods. The Mashantuckets believe Schemitzun is an opportunity not only to share Native cultures and traditions but also to commemorate earlier times when Native Americans helped European settlers stave off starvation by teaching them to grow crops like corn and squash.

The Blessing of the Fleet

Each summer a day is set aside in Stonington for counting blessings, as the commercial fishing fleet there remembers those who have been lost to the sea and prays for safety each time they cast off, earning their livings catching fluke, porgies, sea bass, scallops, and lobster.

Arthur Medeiros is the president of the local fishermen's association. He says he "knew 90 percent of the local men" lost at sea whose names are now engraved on a granite memorial in the village. When Arthur helped initiate the blessing of the fleet in 1954, it was a simple affair, but it has grown into a two-day celebration of the fishing fleet and its heritage, which includes a festival, a concert, a parade through the borough, a memorial Mass, and a parade of boats to be blessed.

Skipper Bob Guzzo's freshly painted and fringe-bedecked boat the *Jenna Lynn* is nestled into a place of honor along the town dock. The *Jenna Lynn* carries the bishop of Norwich, the Most Reverend

Michael Cote, two lace-cassocked priests, and eight altar boys and girls for the religious blessing.

"It's mainly a celebration if we don't lose anybody, and for good luck during the year. Anybody that we did lose—well, that's what it's all about, to

show we love and remember them," Bob explains as he helps guests onto his deck. "And to remember that we do have a big fishing community and fleet in Connecticut."

Carl, Bob's father, a retired carpenter from Bloomfield, thinks of the time he almost lost his son, when Bob's boat struck something in deep water and rapidly went down. "But luckily the water wasn't too cold," Carl says, "and they were rescued by helicopter and boat."

His son chuckles and adds, "What's the big deal? It's only water. Dad was more upset than I was."

Mary Ann Griffin's two sons, Joe and Bill Gilbert, fish, and she proudly calls them "the best in the fleet." But that doesn't mean she doesn't worry. "They grew up on Long Island Sound, both of them. From when they were little, they were both out there," she says. "They used to go fishing before they went to school."

Joe, who hauls about two thousand pounds of sea scallops a day, notes that his mom calls frequently "to remind me to put on my life jacket."

His brother Bill adds, "We do take a moment out to mourn for those who have gone before us, but you can't dwell on it. If you did, you wouldn't go out."

The men are reminded of the danger inherent in commercial fishing by a memorial at the flagpole on Front Street with the names of thirty-five local men who have been lost at sea since 1900.

The bishop of Norwich, resplendent in gold vestments and his white miter, sprinkles holy water on each vessel as it passes the *Jenna Lynn*, saying, "We wish that God would protect all of the men and women who go to sea. This is an honor and it is good to have this opportunity to bless the fleet and pray to keep them safe."

Many of the boats are decorated for the occasion, with fringe, palm trees, and even mermaids and bands on board. They fly the Connecticut, U.S., Portuguese, and Italian flags. Joy and solemnity mingle on deck. After the bishop blesses each vessel, they all steam out of the harbor to a point where one fisherman's body was discovered. A family member tosses a floral wreath in the shape of a broken anchor into the sea, while members of the borough's fire department shoot an eighteen-gun salute in his honor.

Joe Gilbert puts it this way: "We do think about the lost fishermen, but that's part of the business. . . . We take our chances. But if you are good at it, and Mother Nature smiles on you, you do quite well."

Natural Wonders

People often ask me why I commute from our home near Long Island Sound to the Hartford area to work. The answer boils down to this: the view. Tom and I live on an inlet that opens up into Long Island Sound. Our lives are measured by this natural wonder, timed to the rhythms of the tide. In June the marsh grasses start poking above the water's surface—suddenly turn brightly, then brilliantly green. That's when we generally spot the first batch of newly hatched ducklings being ushered about by nervous mothers.

Soon it's time to get our boat in the water for the season. It's perfect for beaching on the Norwalk Islands, right after the terns' nesting season is over and beachcombers can reclaim these small fragments of sand, stone, and beach grass with their hidden coves and safe anchorages. As the days begin to lengthen, evening sailboat races begin at clubs along the coast from Pawcatuck to Greenwich.

Early summer is ripe with anticipation as gardeners prepare their soil to plant their favorite varieties, or simply to feed their families. And the gates to secret gardens swing open for public tours that benefit museums and historical societies. At Farmington's Hill-Stead, for instance, the sunken garden was designed by Beatrix Farrand, who created landscapes for Yale, Princeton, and the White House. At the Glebe House Museum in Woodbury, the gardens designed by Gertrude Jekyll—called the greatest gardener of the twentieth century—have been restored; at the Bellamy-Ferriday House in Bethlehem, the formal garden's design was inspired by the patterns of the family's antique Oriental carpet. The fragrance at Elizabeth Park when its thousands of roses are in bloom rivals the most expensive perfume poured into a bottle, and its cascading blossoms form a kaleidoscope of extravagant hues.

In July Connecticut days are sultry, sending us in search of shore breezes, icy dips in local lakes, or hiking in the green shade of the forest, along trails in state parks with names like Devil's Hopyard. The languid evenings are made for stargazing, on a blanket in your own backyard or at one of the state's observatories. August in Connecticut is voluptuous, with her rolling hills washed in green and stone walls framing cows and horses. Streams and rivers fill to the banks, while fishermen in waders cast for trout.

By Any Other Name

Geraldine Gunnels has come to Elizabeth Park to get ideas for a climbing rose for her garden.

She has a lot to look at: There are fifteen thousand bushes blooming here, with between 750 and 900 varieties of roses. Fences of climbing roses provide a fragrant backdrop.

"It's just absolutely enchanting. It makes me wish that I had something like this at home," Geraldine says.

Three hundred thousand people a year visit Elizabeth Park, which straddles the Hartford–West Hartford city line. The rose garden has been here for a century. As the first American rose garden built with public funds, it is on the National Register of Historic Places. Workshops, tours, sales, and other special events are held throughout the year, but of course it's the warm months when the site explodes with color—and visitors.

The main garden shows off modern roses. Older varieties are planted in the Heritage Garden. Since 1937 this has been a test garden for the American Rose Society, which tries out new varieties here before they are sold to the public. But for a time in the 1970s, the park was dropped from the list of test gardens; city budget cuts meant less care for the

roses, and the weeds grew nearly as tall as the bushes. That's when local garden clubs pitched in, donating time, labor, and thousands of dollars to bring the park back to its prime. Friends of Elizabeth Park was formed, and Donna Fuss, the rosarian for the park, helped restore the gardens to their former splendor.

Although Donna has visited the park regularly for more than fifty years, when she rounds the corner and sees the rose-covered arches in bloom, "it's still very exciting," she declares. "Even if you are not a rose person, it just takes your breath away."

The seventy-two arches are at their peak in late June, swarming with rambling roses like Excelsa, Dorothy Perkins, and White Dorothy.

"I love the rose garden," says retired park foreman John Cosman. "I attribute most of the way the garden looks to the tremendous dedication of the gardeners." A crew of professionals and volunteers tenderly care for their charges. Pruning correctly is important, John explains. "You cut back to your first five-leaf cluster and a new rose will develop right at that point."

John's favorite is a German variety that blooms in bouquets of crimson. Some visitors search for the fuchsia-and-white rose called Love or the palest yellow petals tinged in pink of Peace, the lipstick red of Show Biz, the lemon yellow of Midas Touch, the soft mauve of Blueberry Hill, or the showy coral number called Cary Grant.

On a day so rare in June, the garden inspires watercolor artists who have set up easels beside the row of flower-covered arches. "I just love the roses, and they're all here. There are so many clusters of roses. The colors are magnificent," says one woman while painting.

The Elizabeth Park Rose Garden, a stunning work of nature and loving gardeners, is a city treasure.

REMARKABLE GARDENS

CLOCKWISE FROM TOP LEFT: FORMAL BEDS AND A GREENHOUSE, ONE OF THE SITES ON THE DISCOVERY IN THE GARDEN TOUR, FAIRFIELD; GARDENS BY THE SEA, A STONINGTON WALKING TOUR; COTTAGE GARDEN IN CHESTER; AN ELEGANT POOL ON THE GREENWICH GARDEN TOUR OFFERED BY THE GARDEN EDUCATION CENTER; ROSES TUMBLE OVER A FENCE ON MIDDLE BEACH ROAD IN MADISON; EDGERTON PARK, NEW HAVEN.

The Secret Gardens

Garden tours are held throughout Connecticut in spring and summer, many of them raising funds for nonprofit organizations. One recent year, for instance, a dramatic home and garden were revealed in the Discovery in the Garden Tour in **Fairfield**. Stepping into the palatial European-style stone chateau of Liz and John Petti is a bit like being whisked away to Provence or Tuscany. Their courtyards, terraces, and orchards flow from the home into the eight-acre hillside landscape, dotted with streams, ponds, expansive gardens, and secret places to hide away in the shade with a book. The garden is 90 percent organic, with no spraying done at the estate. "We're not afraid of dandelions," says Liz, though hardly a one can been seen on a stroll through her spacious lawns. The apple orchard provides enough fruit for five hundred pies each year, mostly donated to shelters and fund-raisers for community groups.

One fund-raiser featured a rare glimpse of Martha Stewart's gardens in **Westport.** Eight acres surrounding her 1805 farmhouse are planted with lush beds of poppies, irises, and peonies. "The structure is formal, with straight paths and everything straight and perpendicular or parallel," Martha says. "Yet the gardens themselves are masses of color. It's kind of wild looking when they are all in full bloom."

Martha's love of fine food is evident in her vegetable garden, where more than fifteen varieties of lettuce grow alongside fifty herbs. There are also dozens of varieties of antique roses, countless poppies, and thirty types of alum, commonly known as flowering onions. The garden is a veritable United Nations of irises, with German, Siberian, and Japanese varieties blooming side by side. Describing Martha Stewart's garden as a "good thing" is a bit of an understatement. An "amazing thing" is more like it.

Many other amazing gardens await across the state as well. Contact your local garden center for green spots to tour near you.

Seeds of Hope

There's something healing about working in a garden, nurturing and breathing life into small tomato and potato plants. For some of those gardeners at the Larry Kolp Garden Plots in Farmington, it means even more.

They have lived through horrors unimaginable to most people, but when they came to Connecticut they found a community that cared, and they found a friend in Al Malpa.

"Every one of these people has lost their homes, family, or friends to the war. They came here and it would be like us getting dropped suddenly into China, or someplace very unlike Connecticut," Al remarks. "The real problem is they have no 'Connecticut skills,' which are different than the rest of the U.S. They come from either an agrarian or industrial community, they don't speak the language, plus they've just had this terrible trauma. Some have been in a refugee camp for over a year."

Al owns a construction business, volunteers for the Salvation Army, and is a Rotary member. With the aid of those organizations, he found a way to help war refugees help themselves to a new life and a new outlook. "There just seemed to have been a

seed in Connecticut to reach out to help," Al says with a warm smile.

In a sense he means that literally. Families who escaped the war crimes of Bosnia, Kosovo, or Sierra Leone not only find the culture vastly different here, but often find feeding their families pretty expensive, too. "The problem is they don't have command

of language so they are stuck doing eight- and ten-dollar-an-hour jobs," he says. A former plant manager and a former history professor in Kosovo are now working as baggers at a local supermarket.

So Al thought having their own vegetable gardens would help. With aid from the Salvation Army and Rotary, Al rented fifty-by-fifty-foot garden plots from the town of Farmington, which makes space available to people from all over, including many from urban areas in Hartford, New Britain, Bloomfield, and Newington.

On sign-up day Al arrives at town hall at one in the morning so he can rent half a dozen plots in close proximity. "You see a lotta the same people every year, probably because it's a fabulous deal and a lovely place to be, right along the Farmington River. There are a lot of retirees. They spend a few hours gardening and then sit out here and enjoy the area and the company. It's become a community."

Al's plots all go to war refugees like Kadir and Sena Becirovic, who escaped from Bosnia five years ago with their children, eleven-year-old Dennis and seven-year-old Lejla. On a sunny July morning, Sena remembers the garden she tended in another life and another place, back home. She is a little worried about this summer's plantings. "Everything is small because we had a lot of rain early in the summer."

As she weeds, her husband, Kadir, laughs and teases her. "I do all the work and she bosses me around." Sena giggles.

Their smiles mask the pain they have suffered, being uprooted and then separated for eighteen months. Little Dennis and Sena had been evacuated to relative safety in Tuzla, but Kadir was forced to stay behind. "He had no money, no food, no work, and soldiers wouldn't let them leave," Sena says quietly, after some urging. "One day I am home in Tuzla and I hear somebody say about eighteen men are coming, and I say 'Oh God, please maybe my husband come.' He walked for seven days at night only, so no Serbian soldiers would see him, and he had to hide in the woods during the day. He no have shoes, only maybe socks, and no clothes, except something someone made him from a blanket."

After seeing family and friends killed, the Becirovics fled. Sena and Kadir settled in Hartford, found jobs, and eventually bought a house where they live with other relatives.

Since they all have legal status and working papers, Al helps some of the refugees find work on his contracting projects, or doing odd jobs for homeowners in the Farmington Valley. "Their work ethic is like nothing I have ever seen. They always far exceed whatever we expect to get done. They are so focused," he says with admiration.

And they are generous. "They are always trying to give me their vegetables. I keep saying Sena, no no, you need them for your family. Last weekend I went up to see my mother and they said, 'Oh please, take it for your mother.' You would think that they weren't struggling," he says. "These are happy people in spite of the horror they have seen."

The Becirovic family still has ties to their old life, but they are busy making a new one here—with a little help from some friends and a handful of seeds.

The Basis of Life

It's no wonder Old Wethersfield is home to Comstock, Ferre & Co., the longest continuously operating seed company in this country.

The river town's reputation for seeds is almost as old as Wethersfield itself, which was founded in 1634. The area is blessed with fertile soil, enriched by the annual flooding of the Connecticut River. The Wethersfield Seed Company opened in 1820 and expanded when Franklin Comstock and Henry Ferre took over not long after. Stephen Willard began working for Comstock Ferre in 1871, the first of four generations of Willards to run the business.

"We are dealing with a basic commodity," says Corinne Willard: "the basis of life." Most of our food comes directly from seeds. And as far as flower seeds are concerned, well, we certainly need beauty in our lives."

In 1947 horticulturist Corinne Willard married her husband, Dick. His family's business clearly influenced their honeymoon: "We spent it in what they call a corn nursery in Idaho, testing new varieties of sweet corn," Corinne reminisces. Two of Corinne and Dick's children went into the seed business, and so did their nephew Ted Willard.

"We sold over 850 varieties of seeds. We carried some older varieties to keep the folks who have been

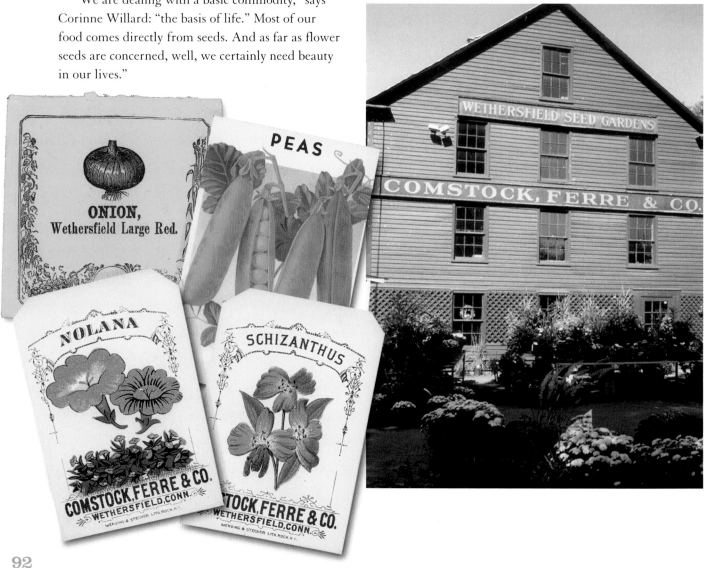

growing a certain variety forever happy," says Ted. "But to be a new introduction to Comstock Ferre, it had to do something better than anything else on the market."

Today Ted runs his own firm called New England Seed Company, and Comstock Ferre has new owners. Still, everything about this place reminds you that Comstock Ferre has been around a long time. The building they call the "new warehouse" went up in 1880. One of the buildings dates back to the mid-1700s and once belonged to Silas Deane, a merchant before the Revolutionary War.

When the company started in the early nineteenth century, it depended on river transportation to distribute consignment boxes of seeds to general stores, where gardeners picked packets of wildflowers and vegetables. Over the years Comstock Ferre turned to wholesaling. But after World War II, Dick Willard recognized a change in society that would directly affect his business.

"It was the time of Levittown. Acres of farmland on Long Island were developed into housing," Dick explained. "Well, when that happened, the business of selling seeds also changed."

Comstock Ferre started catering to backyard gardeners and branched out into floral arranging, plant sales, herbal preparations, and home decor. But the heart of the company remained seeds, tested in the lab and still sold from antique cabinets.

Even after Dick Willard retired, he continued to oversee the greenhouses and trial beds. "I feel that we are helping society," he said. "I wouldn't do it otherwise."

Dick Willard passed away not long ago, but his widow Corinne remains in Wethersfield, and is an avid gardener. "Oh my gosh, yes," she says. "I couldn't do without it. I will garden as long as I can still move!"

We Are
the Champions

Take a look at that quarter in your pocket. If it's a Connecticut quarter, one side features the Charter Oak, a tree that played a big part in the liberty of our land.

In 1687 a representative for King James II challenged Connecticut's government and demanded the surrender of its charter. During a heated discussion, with the charter resting on the table between the opposing sides, the candles were snuffed out. When the room became light again, the Connecticut charter had disappeared. Captain Joseph Wadsworth

had snatched the charter from the British and concealed it in a majestic white oak. The Charter Oak survived until summer 1856.

These days, notable trees like the Charter Oak are still found in the state. Howard Porter is rightfully proud of the three notable trees on his property in Guilford. "I found this one in 1954, when it was

COMMON APPLE, NORTH STONINGTON

94

seven inches high. It grew about three feet a year for a long time," he says, proudly circling one of them, a dawn redwood.

Glenn Dreyer, a Connecticut College botanist and director of the college's arboretum, says Howard's dawn redwood is indeed particularly noteworthy. "They found it in a very out-of-the-way place in China. All the seeds that came into this country came from one small stand in China."

In Essex there's another tree that came a long way—a ninety-foot-tall pagoda tree. "That's a tree native to Asia," explains Glenn. "Essex and New London were seafaring towns. The captains would bring interesting plants home from their voyages."

In Waterford a blue Atlas cedar graces the lawn of the police department, and it is something of a rarity in the state. "That tree is marginally hardy in Connecticut. For the most part it will only grow in the warmer parts of the state, near the coastline, where Waterford is," explains Glenn.

In 1985, with the founding of the Connecticut Notable Trees Project, Glenn led a dedicated group of volunteer botanists in compiling a list of the champion trees in the state. To make the list a tree had to either be the biggest of its species or be historically significant. "It's very species dependent," he says. "For instance, the Washington hawthorn we have around the other side of the pond here at the arboretum is just three feet in circumference, and it's as big as the national champion. It has been a national co-champion tree."

It's uncommon to find trees in Connecticut that are more than 150 years old. Much of our land was cleared for farming in the 1800s, with its trees felled for firewood and building materials. Still, some trees are huge and several centuries old. A sugar maple in Norwich was once denoted the biggest in the country—which also makes it the biggest in the world, since sugar maples are only known to grow here. The tree is twenty-two feet around and more than ninety-three feet tall.

The most historic tree in Connecticut, after the Charter Oak, was the Washington Oak in Gaylordsville, a hamlet of New Milford. The tree was believed to be as much as four hundred years old when it perished in 2003. It was said to have been the

SYCAMORE, SIMSBURY

place where George Washington stopped not once but twice during the Revolutionary War. The Daughters of the American Revolution, who long cared for the tree, claimed that Washington met beneath its shade in 1780 with the marquis de Lafayette during a trip to Hartford to enlist other French officers in the war against England. At one time the tree measured some eighty feet tall and twenty-four feet in circumference, with a canopy spread of 115 feet. When the white oak succumbed, Jennie Rehnberg, the regent of the Roger Sherman Chapter of the DAR, was devastated: "A part of our history is lost and it cannot be recaptured." The DAR hopes to plant a sapling from an acorn from the Washington Oak so a new tree might grow in its place.

Two trees from Connecticut are currently on the list of national notable trees, and more have recently been submitted for consideration. If you have a tree you think could make the list, try to identify its species, then measure its circumference at a point four and a half feet from the ground. You can submit the information to the Connecticut College Arboretum, 270 Mohegan Avenue, Box 5201, New London 06320. You just might find a new Connecticut champion!

NATURE IN HER
MANY MOODS

CLOCKWISE FROM TOP LEFT: IN THE

MARSHES OF GUILFORD; BATTERSON PARK

IN FARMINGTON; SUNFLOWERS IN GRISWOLD;

A TRAIL THROUGH DEVIL'S HOPYARD IN EAST

HADDAM; LONG ISLAND SOUND ACTS UP AT

HAMMONASSET BEACH STATE PARK, MADI-

SON; BUOYS IN EAST HADDAM.

The Black Dog of Meriden

The Hanging Hills of Meriden host Hubbard Park, an 1,800-acre recreation area that offers a picnic pavilion, a playground for children, and tennis courts. The hills are renowned for their gorges and unusual rock formations, which attract both recreational hikers and geologists, and for the unusual stone tower known as Castle Craig. Yet perhaps the hills' greatest claim to fame is their ghostly black dog.

Eastern Connecticut State University professor David Philips, the late author of *Legendary Connecticut*, told the story: "Many who have visited the Hanging Hills have seen the black dog—a shorthaired, sad-eyed beast looking vaguely like a spaniel," Dave intoned. "Nothing exceptional about him, except that whether he is seen in the snows of winter or the dust of summer, he leaves no paw prints; and although he appears to bark, no sound is ever heard."

There is a local saying, according to Dave: "If a man shall meet the black dog once, it shall be for joy; if twice, it shall be for sorrow; and the third time, he shall die."

The legend was strengthened by a report pub-lished in an 1898 issue of *Connecticut Quarterly*. Said Dave, "A New York geologist named W. H. C. Pynchon arrived in Meriden to study the rock forma-tions and encountered the black dog, which he found an amiable companion for the day." Several years later Pynchon returned with a colleague who mentioned that on two earlier trips, he had also seen the black dog. The two made their climb the next day, "and they saw him, the small black dog each had seen before, wagging his tail. But before reaching the spaniel above them on a ledge, Pynchon's companion slipped and fell to his death hundreds of feet below. The prophecy had been fulfilled."

Warming to telling his story, Dave then delivered the punch line. "Although that detail ended his article in the magazine, it wasn't the end of Pynchon's tale. He would make one more trip to Meriden, and, in retracing the route taken with his friend, he too slipped and plunged to his death."

So when hiking the Hanging Hills high above Meriden, enjoy the spectacular views—and watch out for black dogs.

Star Power

For much of his life, Monty Robeson has either been in the sky or staring up at it. An airline pilot, Monty has seen the wonders of the universe unfold around him.

"One late night coming from Las Vegas to Dallas, there was a meteor shower. It was really intense," he recalls. "It was very special, and something that I'd never seen before. All the meteors seemed to be coming straight down, vertically down."

As an amateur astronomer, the New Milford man has long been inspired by the stars. So when his town began building a new forty-eight-million dollar high school, Monty decided the school needed one thing more—a place for stargazers. He and a team of volunteers set out to build a first-class observatory, one of the finest on any public school campus in the nation.

Alexandra Thomas, chair of the board of education, remembers when Monty and his friends first broached the idea with the board in 1998. "They were speaking about things that we had no idea about," says Alexandra. "Most people hadn't even been in an observatory, so they were speaking a foreign language at first."

What the board *did* understand was that Monty and his friends were offering the town an opportunity, and that they were willing to do all the work and raise all the money to make it happen. All they asked from the board was permission and a location near the new high school.

Their goal was bigger than teaching kids about the stars. "The young people coming up really have to be literate in science if for no other reason than to make good decisions at the polling places," says Monty. "They need to have a background in science and the logical thinking that goes along with it."

A group of about twenty formed a nonprofit organization, the Western Connecticut Chapter of the Society for Amateur Scientists. It took them two years to raise a quarter of a million dollars from private foundations, the state, the local government, local businesses, even schoolkids and their families. They built community support, and even got the construction materials donated. All the while Jeff Miskie worked on the design.

"Last I counted it was about fourteen different major revisions of a floor plan before we finally arrived at this design," Jeff says with a chuckle. "Even during construction we were making last-minute modifications and changes in what we call 'creative carpentry.'"

For seven months the volunteers toiled tirelessly, doing most of the construction themselves. "The hours were, I've got to admit, pretty long," Jeff recalls. "We'd get off work, race down here right away just to start slinging nails till ten, eleven, twelve o'clock at night. Many of us spent our vacations down here and a lot of our free time, including weekends."

They built a facility open to everyone, regardless of physical limitations. Cub Scout Will Hermann makes good use of the wheelchair lift and a fiber-optic eyepiece extender, custom-designed so anyone can get a look at the skies.

One large telescope and the other two piggy-backed on it are operated by keypad, or by computer. So is the motorized dome. Eventually a visitor from anywhere in the world will be able to control the telescopes via the Internet. The scopes are tied into cameras that allow amateur scientists and students to capture images for further study. Images are fed into the observatory's second room, or directly into the high school.

What's the appeal of the summer sky? For some,

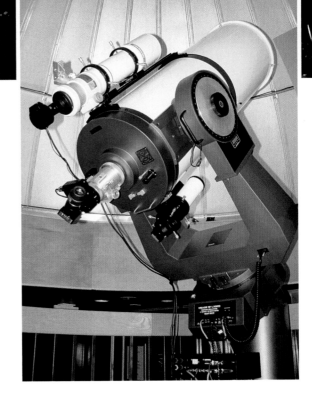

a visit is an opportunity to reflect on the universe and our place in it. Asked why it's so fascinating to stare into the night, one stargazer replied: "We're just wondering what's up there and we don't know yet. It's basic curiosity."

The International Astronomical Union assigned code number 932 to the McCarthy Observatory. Since codes are earned only by facilities that produce astronomical measurements of the highest quality, that was a benchmark, a sign of excellence. But these New Milford citizens have accomplished even more: They have shown their neighbors what volunteers can do for their community.

Creatures from the Deep

More than half a million people visit the Maritime Aquarium in the SoNo section of Norwalk each year, and I am usually one of them. But one of my encounters there seemed a bit daunting.

"Would you like to pet a shark?" asked aquarist Tom Ford. With visions of *Jaws* dancing through my head, I thought the appropriate answer was, "Are you kidding? Do I want to lose an arm? No, I don't think so!"

But Tom comforted me with the facts. "There are 350 different species of sharks out there. Only five of them are hazardous to people."

As I approached the touch tank, I wondered if this would be the first documented attack by a spotted bamboo shark. Encouraged when my hand

emerged with the same number of fingers I had plunked into the water, I felt bold enough to stroke the cow nose ray that kept peeking above the surface of the water, with eyes that reminded me of my spaniel at home.

The touch tank is just one part of a gallery that explores what fish are all about. "You're bigger and stronger than a striped bass, but a striped bass can swim faster than you can. Why is that?" asks Dave Sigworth, a media specialist at the aquarium. "It's because of the way the fish is shaped. We also want visitors to think about how a fish sees—because a fish sees differently than you or me—and how they breathe oxygen in the water, why they don't drown."

The aquarium is devoted to exploring and understanding the body of water we live closest to—Long Island Sound. Its twenty habitats contain more than a thousand animals and represent life from tidal pools to the depths of the Atlantic, including oysters, jellyfish, sea horses, small fish, rays, and nine-foot sand tiger sharks.

The five harbor seals are the showstoppers, especially at feeding time, and the matriarch of the group, Suzie, is about to celebrate her thirtieth birthday. Since the aquarium opened in 1988 in a former nineteenth-century iron works factory, an expansion has allowed the animal collection to grow. It now includes two loggerhead sea turtles each weighing well over two hundred pounds. River

otters Belle and Lew cavort playfully in their tank. Although about a thousand otters live in the wild in Connecticut, you rarely catch a glimpse of one since they are generally only active at dawn and at dusk.

The aquarium's research vessel offers cruises to groups and individuals nearly year-round. You'll also find boatbuilding classes and a new educational building with high-tech classrooms for student scientists. All in all this watery wonderland is an ideal summer outing.

REMARKABLE FLORA AND FAUNA

CLOCKWISE FROM TOP LEFT: BARTLETT ARBORETUM IN STAMFORD; EGRET IN STAMFORD; COMMON TERN AT FAULKNER ISLAND, GUILFORD; WOOD LILY IN NEHANTIC STATE FOREST; A CRAB CLAMBERS OVER A PEBBLY BEACH IN STONINGTON. FACING PAGE: A FROG PLUCKED FROM THE MARSHES OF HAMMONASSET IN MADISON.

A Reverence for Stone

Stone by stone—that's how a mason builds a wall.

Stone by Stone is also the name of the book that has been called a manifesto on the history of New England's stone walls. Its author, UConn geology professor Robert "Thor" Thorson, moved to Connecticut from Alaska. He remembers, "The first time I stepped out into the woods and I saw a stone wall surrounded by trees growing up in the woods, it struck me that it was a *ruin*. I have been attached to stone walls in sort of an interesting way ever since."

In communities like Hebron, the locations of stone walls now appear on survey information filed by developers with town planner Mike O'Leary. "It's in response to the town saying 'these are significant elements of the landscape.' We want to see if we can work those into the final design so they're preserved," he explains. "We find that developers are responding very well to that."

As homes go up, old stone walls like the pair lining what was once a colonial cartway or cattle path are being saved, or if necessary moved and reassembled nearby.

"Hebron, much like a lot of towns in eastern Connecticut, has a rural history, an agricultural history. Stone walls are very often the fabric of the community, the part of the community I think people recognize and enjoy and want to maintain," says Mike.

Thor says that's one element in an equation that makes Connecticut perhaps the epicenter of stone walls. "To be what I call 'signatures of the landscape' you need three things in place," he believes. "One of them has to be a livestock farming economy, because you need to clear the trees; because you need to have animals on the land. You need to be haying and taking care of property where fences matter."

And, he goes on, "You have to have glaciated soils, and the glaciated soils have to have a third element: They have to have hard, slabby crystalline rocks. If they don't, then the stones are crushed by the glacier."

Professor Thorson is concerned about what he sees as the theft and sale of stone walls to property owners who want to bring a bit of New England to their plot of land, no matter where they live. "People are willing to pay quite a bit of money for it, and so stones are being strip mined and solicited for strip mining off otherwise beautiful abandoned farmsteads," he laments. "Often that stone is going to places where the stone doesn't even look right. In fact, it looks sort of crude or ostentatious or architecturally out of place."

New Englanders are noticing, taking interest, and taking action. Thorson's two books, *Stone by Stone* and the children's book *Stone Wall Secrets,* have led to a grant to develop a school curriculum based on stone walls.

"It would be the node to which literature, to which history, to which science and math attach. Because there's plenty of mathematics here," he says, pointing to a stone wall along a country road. "We can talk about dimensions of height, width, size, weight and mass, straightness and curvature, and all of that. There's also plenty of history here, as cultural heritage about Yankee farmers and early colonists and pioneers. And I would argue that stone walls are known better in literature than anywhere else, through poetry and through imagery."

Professor Thorson believes we have what he calls a "reverence for stone" because "it is a way to connect back to the founding of our country. Not just the founding of New England, but of our whole country."

Fields of Dreams

With two Belgian draft horses tilling his field, Ernie Staebner looks like a man who has stepped out of the past. Farmers have worked this land in Franklin since before the Revolutionary War.

"We need to spend some more time with what happened years ago, or it's gonna be lost," Ernie says. "Is it important or not important to know what happened years ago? I think it is important to know what happened." So important that this is no longer only a 385-acre working dairy farm, but also home to the Blue Slope Country Museum.

It started when Ernie's dad passed away, leaving behind a collection of four thousand farm tools dating from 1700 to 1950. "Instead of leaving them in the attic in boxes like so many people do, we thought it would be nice to display them, so we could play with them and our friends could come and do something with them," according to Ernie. "Then one day someone said, 'Why don't you make a museum out of it?'" Soon his wife, Sandy, was stitching up colonial costumes and recruiting family and friends for special events.

Thirteen-year-old granddaughter Rebecca demonstrates an antique loom for visitors. "If I was the oldest daughter in the house I would spend most

of the day working on the loom for six hours a day or more," she explains.

Janice Steinhagen chimes in from her seat at a spinning wheel nearby. "I have heard tell that it's the origin of the word *spinster*. The oldest daughter in the family would be the person who was responsible for churning out the amount of yarn that the mother would need to clothe the family, and as a result she was too busy to court anyone."

Eleven-year-old Allison Kneser is visiting from Phillipsburg, New Jersey. "It was neat how they showed us all the stuff they used back in the older days," she says.

Sandy Staebner is glad to hear that reaction. "It's very gratifying when you can watch young people come back year after year and they've really absorbed some of the agricultural history that we've tried to share with them."

But for Sandy and Ernie, this is about more than the past; it's about the future of farming in Connecticut. "The children don't realize the cow has to have a calf to make milk," Sandy says, because children think the milk comes from the grocery store. *"We don't need farmers! There's plenty of food in the A&P!* We've heard it, we've been told that."

That's why former state agriculture commissioner Shirley Ferris heavily promotes agritourism. "I think it's really important to get the public *with* the farmer. There needs to be some interaction," Shirley says. "Too often our generation has gotten so far from the land, people don't have an understanding of the value of what's around them."

A map guides people to farms all over Connecticut that welcome visitors. In a state that loses eight thousand acres of farmland a year, tourism may

boost some struggling farms. "The dollars that can be garnered by selling your land to a housing developer or to industrial or commercial development are very tempting, I'm sure," admits Shirley, the wife of a farmer. The state agriculture department has also promoted a farmland preservation act to save some of Connecticut's rural charm as well as its local source of food.

"We have to keep repeating this story that agriculture is important," Sandy Staebner echoes. "It's important to keep this land not just so it looks pretty but so it can produce food for people."

Let's Play

Summer is playtime in Connecticut. Venus and Serena Williams dominate the Pilot Pen Tennis Tournament in New Haven, the gallery at the Tournament Players Club is always jammed when the professional golf tour rolls into Cromwell, and our minor-league ballparks highlight the stars of tomorrow—as well as glimpses of marquee pitchers working their way back to the big leagues while recovering from injuries. Independence Day weekend brings old-fashioned baseball, played the way it was when the game began, with "ballists" garbed in woolen uniforms, politely addressing the straw-hat-wearing umpire as "sir." Our state has a long baseball history; even Mark Twain was a big fan!

The sparkle of Connecticut's waters on a sunny day offer another alluring playground. Sail the seas on a schooner, or meet marine life from the depths aboard a floating laboratory. It's good to know that when every manner of craft takes to the deep, from Jet Skis to Hobie cats to yachts, dedicated volunteers are there to lend a hand just in case. Sea kayaking, river rafting, or just floating down the Farmington in a tube on a hot summer's day are for those who like to get really wet. Or you can take in the view from water skis on one of the many lakes dotting our state.

Ronald Reagan often said, "There's nothing better for the inside of a man than the outside of a horse." For some that means riding through woodland trails and open meadows, but for others horseshoes are for tossing at stakes in a town that's been the horseshoe capital of Connecticut for decades. Bowlers gather on green lawns for a game that dates back to ancient times.

A few years ago I rediscovered the joy of pedaling along a quiet country road and soaking in details of the landscape that I often miss when they whiz by during a car ride. It's a solitary pastime that seems to go best with summer's warm breezes and lush landscapes.

The Boys
of Summer

The good old days are back: the days when baseball was a gentleman's game, the days before bench-clearing brawls, sky-high salaries, big-time footwear endorsements, and suspicions of steroid use.

Nineteenth-century baseball is being resurrected, and it's expanding with new teams playing each season.

One of the biggest tournaments of the year is the brainchild of Greg "Moonlight" Martin, who plays for the Hartford Senators. He describes the sport as "unique baseball, history, theater, and competitive play" all wrapped up together.

Greg ballyhoos his Hartford Vintage Base Ball Invitational over the Independence Day weekend in Bushnell Park as "Three Days. Twelve Clubs. Twenty Games. One Champion." The teams travel from New York, New Jersey, Connecticut, Rhode Island, and Massachusetts.

The hometown team is dressed in woolen uniforms designed for the Hartford Senators to wear in 1923, although on this day temperatures are hovering in the nineties. Mark Winowski, a spectator from Hartford, says, "I play softball and I would love to get into this. But you know what, they are wearing wool, so I don't know. It's almost ninety-two degrees right now. They look warm!"

Greg points out that the uniforms are adapted from the glory days of the original Hartford Senators, who played from 1902 to 1934. In 1923 Lou Gehrig played his only season of minor-league ball with the team before his call up to the big leagues and the New York Yankees.

At 10:00 A.M. the players are warming up. Team captain Chris Moran is already perspiring profusely. But he says gamely, "What's motivating us is that Sam Adams beer truck over there. Two hours from

now we will be enjoying cool refreshment."

That will be after two hours of playing a game dramatically different from the one we know today. Vintage teams play by rules set in the 1860s or the 1880s, and the evolution of the game unfolds on the field, where trees in the outfield are not only acceptable, they're playable.

"It's much more challenging than softball because many people don't use any gloves. Those who do use these small suede work gloves," first baseman Rob Miller of Coventry explains, donning something that looks more like a gardening glove than a baseball mitt. "The era when we play is right when they were transitioning from no gloves to leather work gloves or whatever else they had lying around the cabin." When he's not playing vintage baseball, Rob is the director of public health for a five-town area.

The games played by the earliest rules feature slow underhanded pitching. On this sunny day, the Senators, once a favorite team of Mark Twain, are taking on the Providence Grays, a team wearing uniforms styled in 1884.

Beside a banner that reads NO CURSING, SPITTING OR GAMBLING ALLOWED is another indicating BALLIST ENTRANCE to the field. *Ballist* was the term for the players. Fans were cranks, the games were matches, and the final score was the tally.

Harry Higham is an umpire for a Long Island team called the New York Mutuals, but his history is with Hartford. In 1876 his great-grandfather Dick Higham played for the Hartford Dark Blues. "He

played every position, but mostly catcher," Harry says, pointing to the sepia-toned picture of Dick in a vintage program handed out at the tournament. "His lifetime batting average was .307. He was usually the leadoff hitter." The revived Dark Blues are also competing in the tournament, which features almost nonstop action for three days.

Players on the Hartford squad hail from as near as an apartment overlooking Bushnell Park to as far away as New Hampshire. Steve Soba, director of admissions for Southern New Hampshire University, is a recent convert from softball to vintage baseball. "I had a friend in the area and when that guy left town, I was stuck with these fellas." Steve laughs while other Senators slap him on the back. "I love baseball and I have been playing it forever. I stumbled across this last year and stuck with it. It's a lot of fun."

And a lot of people seem to be discovering that. The number of teams is growing, with more than 150 vintage teams nationwide.

Rob Miller explains the appeal. "At some point I sort of lost interest in softball. Greg noticed that there were some teams playing with unique uniforms and unique rules and asked our softball team if we wanted to convert to vintage baseball. So a couple of us tried it and had a good time doing it. The rest is history—literally!"

Also history in today's baseball are the manners players were expected to adhere to in the early days of the game, including cheering for ballists on the

opposing team. "Nice wood, Charlie," they shout after a player for the Grays hits a long ball into the outfield. "Too bad you hit it right at him," they console as the "sky ball" (now know as a pop-up fly) is caught by their own outfielder. The umpire, dressed in a straw boater and suit, is referred to as "sir." If a player is called safe when he knows better, he is obliged to call himself out.

Displays off the field show the evolution of bats, which started out shaped more like wooden paddles, and balls, which bounce a bit because of their rubber core.

It's not your father's style of baseball, nor even your grandfather's, but vintage baseball on a summer's day is a sport worth reviving.

The Bears, the Bees, and the Blues

inor-league baseball's Bridgeport Bluefish have revived a long tradition of baseball in this seacoast city.

Professional baseball was being played here not long after the invention of the game. The biggest local star was a hometown boy named Jim O'Rourke, whose nickname was "The Orator" and who is Bridgeport's only entry in the Baseball Hall of Fame in Coopers-town. A Yale-educated lawyer, O'Rourke played every position on the team and still holds the record as the oldest man ever to play in the National League. (He was fifty-four!) O'Rourke is believed to be the only man to play in four decades—the 1870s, 1880s, 1890s, and the 1900s. He had the very first hit in the National League and became the highest-paid player of his time while leading the New York Giants to two world championships. Baseball lore has it that he once chewed out an umpire, and then he fined himself for it!

He's also credited with the demise of handlebar mustaches in baseball, after his whipped into his eyes and he missed an easy fly ball. Today, you can see O'Rourke's former home from I–95 North, a solitary Queen Ann house in the middle of fifty acres of open land in Bridgeport's "Steel Point." When everything else was razed at the site, O'Rourke's home was untouched, because baseball lovers and historians hope to restore it and turn it into a Con-necticut Baseball Hall of Fame.

In the 1920s Hall of Famer Ed Walsh moved to the city to manage the Bridgeport Bears. "It was an Eastern League team that played other cities on the East Coast. In the 1940s the Bees came to Bridgeport," notes Barbara Kram, formerly the execu-tive director of the Barnum Museum. "They didn't get too much fame or notori-ety but they had a good time. Bridgeport always supported baseball."

And the fans were loyal to their players. In the 1950s the team signed second baseman George Handy (photo above) from the Negro Leagues, and he became the toast of the town. So when the Bluefish take the field at The Ball Park at Harbor Yard, the boys of this summer are tied to an enduring Bridgeport legacy.

PROFESSIONAL SPORTING EVENTS FILL THE SUMMER.

CLOCKWISE FROM TOP LEFT: THE NORWICH NAVIGATORS PLAY AT DODD STADIUM AT SUNSET; SUZY WHALEY COMPETES IN THE PROFESSIONAL GOLF TOUR IN CROMWELL; TWO TRANS-AM SERIES RACE CARS ROAR ALONG THE TRACK AT LIME ROCK PARK; VENUS WILLIAMS TRIUMPHANT AT THE PILOT PEN TENNIS TOURNAMENT IN NEW HAVEN.

The Sailor's Life for Me

If summer heat's got you bothered and only the spray from a boat can fix it, you're in luck: All manner of watercraft ply the shores, lakes, and rivers of Connecticut.

They range from schooners to riverboat paddle wheelers to sea kayaks, canoes, and inflatable tubes. There are educational cruises, dinner cruises, mystery cruises, even an underground tour of the city of Hartford on the Park River, which was buried as part of a flood control project. Guide boats and kayak tours will take you up close to chains of islands, like the rocky Thimbles or the sandy Norwalk Islands. Step aboard—the state's waters are alive with opportunities.

Learning while having fun is the whole idea of **Schooner Sound Learning,** which offers sailing and

tors trained in marine biology, environmental studies, history, sailing, and education. One young woman is speaking quietly to the children gathered on deck at her feet. "We want to be very careful with the animals that we catch. We call them 'ambassadors.' They are visiting us from the sea while we learn about them. Then we are going to put them back and we don't want to hurt them."

Many of the campers, from the suburbs and the city, shriek as nets are hauled aboard brimming with live creatures. The campers gather around a touch tank for a closer look.

A flounder is gently lifted from the tank on deck, and another instructor points out, "That's the pectoral fin there by my left thumb, and the lateral line goes along there. See how it goes arching up right there?" The children gingerly touch the slippery skin of the fish.

Soon the kids are raising the dark-colored sails while singing a chantey. "In South Australia where I was born, heave away, haul away—bound for South Australia." Small hands reach one above the other as the staysail is hauled into place.

It seems the afternoon has just drifted away in the hazy summer sun, because all too soon the captain shouts, "Prepare to come about." Kids scramble to gently release the remaining critters overboard, and soon the *Quinnipiack*, the flagship of New Haven, is back at her berth at Long Wharf.

Another opportunity for kids or adults interested in knowing more about marine biology and the life of Long Island Sound is the floating classroom operated by **Project Oceanology,** an association of schools and colleges out of Avery Point in Groton. Professional marine scientists will take you aboard *Enviro-Lab* for a two-and-a-half-hour hands-on research cruise, or a visit to New London's famously haunted Ledge Lighthouse—which can only be reached by boat and only explored by permission. Oceancamp is for kids in grades five through twelve.

But there's more—much more. At the western end of Long Island Sound, the scientists from the **Norwalk Maritime Aquarium** conduct hands-on cruises aboard their research vessel *Oceanic.* You'll

marine life programs for adults and kids as young as four years old. Get out on Long Island Sound in their fleet of boats for sailing lessons, sunset picnic cruises, pirate cruises, chantey and ale nights, charter cruises, and—maybe the most popular—educational summer camps for seafaring young scientists.

On a foggy morning in New Haven Harbor, the ninety-one-foot wooden gaff-rigged schooner *Quinnipiack* is pulling away from the dock at Long Wharf, loaded with children and a staff of instruc-

learn about life above and below the surface of the sound. Don't forget your camera, though you may be just as intrigued by what you'll see in the microscope on board. Marine life is collected at all depths, and the trawl net is a harvest of starfish, crabs, fish, and the occasional lobster.

In Stamford the eighty-foot-long tall ship *Sound-Waters* is a replica of a three-masted nineteenth-century Chesapeake Bay sharpie schooner. Its two-hour ecology sails include trawling for creatures that inhabit the underwater world of the sound. The schooner is available for charters for corporate parties, wedding receptions, and other gatherings.

Take a windjammer sailing adventure, from one afternoon to five days in length, aboard the *Mystic Whaler,* a 110-foot replica of the coastal trader of New England from a century ago. The vessel carries three thousand square feet of sail, which you can help raise, or you can simply lie on the deck and nap in the sun and sea breezes. Lengthier sails may include Block Island, Shelter Island, Newport, Sag Harbor, or Martha's Vineyard as ports of call. The Whaler also offers lobster dinner sails, lighthouse cruises, and cruises to New York City and the Chesapeake Bay.

Charters and gift certificates are available.

The **Sunbeam Fleet** in Waterford offers nature cruises, including whale-watching, seal-watching, and eagle-watching in season; deep-sea fishing; even fireworks cruises. If you're a lighthouse lover, you'll get a good look at Saybrook Breakwater, Lynde Point, Pequot, New London Ledge, Morgan Point, Latimer's Reef, North Dumpling, Race Rock, Little Gull, Plum Island, and Orient Point Lighthouses. The boats leave from Captain John's Sport Fishing Center. The owners have been in the boating business for fifty years. Open party boats and charters are available for fishing.

While many of these boats are accessible for people who have disabilities, **Sail Connecticut Access** is a program designed specifically to offer sailing opportunities for people who use wheelchairs or have other physical challenges. The volunteer group has been around since 1989 and gives people with disabilities the chance to enjoy the freedom of the wind and the waves as passengers or as skippers. They sail out of Pilot's Point Marina in Westbrook.

In summer in Connecticut, the waters are beckoning.

America's Volunteer Lifesavers

Since World War II the sailors of Milford-based Coast Guard Flotilla 24-3 have stood at the ready. Part of the Coast Guard Auxiliary—founded in 1939 to assist the regular Coast Guard with non-law-enforcement situations and instruction—the flotilla is staffed entirely by volunteers.

The aftermath of Hurricane Gloria in 1985 may have been the Coast Guard Auxiliary's finest hour. "The marina was pretty well blown away by the wind and high tides. More than twenty-five sailboats were blown aground in the mudflats and backyards off Pond Street. We spent four days salvaging those boats," recalled former Commander Les McPherson before his recent death. Yet the salvage operation was typical of the flotilla. When a boater needs help, the auxiliary is there.

At a practice rescue for 24-3, the rescue boat's captain calls to the "stranded" vessel. "Okay, Skipper, we're going to take you in tow. Please have everybody don PFDs"—personal flotation devices.

The drills are critical because every summer these volunteers assist dozens of boaters—and the numbers are growing. "On a weekend it's so congested it reminds me of Forty-second Street and Broadway. There are over a hundred thousand boats registered in Connecticut of all sizes," Les explained. "Unfortunately many are handled by people with little

experience in boating. In fact, some don't have the vaguest notion except 'turn the key.'"

Safety on the water starts on land, and so the auxiliary offers training courses in safe boating. "We cover all the basic aspects of boating, the rules of the road, engines, proper use of radio and telephone equipment, and of course piloting so people can find their way from one place to another," Les said. In addition, the organization's safe-boat inspections will help you review what you ought to have on board.

The next time you're out on the water, look for the dedicated volunteers of the Coast Guard Auxiliary and tip your hat in thanks.

Up and Away

As the shout goes up, the tethered balloons begin flashing in the dark. It's called a "night glow" and it's how hot-air balloonists from across the state kick off the annual August Plainville Hot Air Balloon Festival, lighting up the sky with a kaleidoscope of color.

Just a few hours later the balloon crews are back in Norton Park before the sun comes up. They work quickly, preparing for the presunrise launch. The nylon "envelopes," as they are called, are spread out, while liquefied propane gas burners are tested, unleashing giant flames into the air. Meanwhile the wicker baskets are prepped and put into place.

"This fan is going to blow air in," says Robert Zirpolo, who runs Berkshire Balloons out of Southington. He explains that the flame will heat the air, causing the balloon to rise.

With the help of a giant fan, the balloon fills with air, lifting the basket upright. First-time passengers have preflight jitters. Paul Michalowski of Cheshire pronounces himself scared. "She's a lot more optimistic," Paul says, pointing to his wife, Penny, who

pronounces herself "really excited about this."

A small balloon is released to determine which way the wind will carry the craft. As the sun rises, so do the balloons. With a burst of flame the basket, carrying seven people, is off the ground and easing into the sky. It's a perfect day for flying, and soon more than thirty balloons are up, up, and away. The festival, which is a fund-raiser for the Plainville Fire Department, is in its second decade.

Skimming the skies in a hot-air balloon allows an intimacy with nature and sometimes with the people living along the flight path. "You can meet people with a balloon!" Robert says. He calls to the folks below who are still in their pajamas on this early summer morning: "How ya doing? Did we wake you up?"

They shout back, "We're doing great. See you later."

Robert is also an airline pilot. "The balloon does move slow; you come in low," he says. "So I can have a conversation with this person in their backyard. You can't do that in an airplane going a hundred miles per hour with an engine blaring."

Traveling above the treetops allows passengers to enjoy the Connecticut countryside in a way most never have before. The wind steers the balloon's course. Soon a line of balloons from the festival is fanning out above the horizon.

Keith Hall is a member of Robert's chase crew. "The whole aerodynamics is different. You go where the wind goes, as opposed to a plane, where you have a lot more control." Which is why a balloon *needs* a chase crew. The pilot has little idea where he will end up, though he can control the landing. So Robert keeps in close contact with his crew, who follow the balloon's every move and assist in launching and landing.

"You have to be familiar with the area," points out Kimberly Goode, another member of the crew. "You want to be there before the balloon gets there or at least about the same time."

Diane Thompson, a passenger from Brookfield, calls her ride "a dream come true."

Penny Michalowski hopes she has converted her husband to a balloon believer. "This is the best thing we've ever done, right, honey? We are going to do this again, aren't we?"

Paul's still not so sure, but he agrees, "Yes, we are."

Soon the voyage is ending, and Robert scouts for a good site to land. This time it's a grassy field at a Cheshire nursery, where greenhouse workers are surprised at the sight of the gracefully descending craft.

After a gentle landing, the chase crew arrives, and everyone pitches in to pack up the balloon. Back in the early days, fuel from the balloons would cover crops with dirty black soot. Farmers weren't always glad to see the balloons, so pilots packed bottles of bubbly as a thank-you for allowing them to land.

That tradition lives on, only now pilots usually return to the site of ascent before making a champagne toast.

So it's cheers to the sport of hot-air ballooning, a way to see the state from a new perspective.

It's a Ringer

S ummer evenings in Deep River enjoy a sleepy solitary quality—except on Thursday, when the quiet is shattered by iron slamming into stakes. In Deep River they've played horseshoes every Thursday night in spring and summer for nearly fifty years.

"I was new to town and the guy who delivered the mail was Al Pearson, the founder of the league," says John Ely, a charter member of the Deep River Horseshoe League. "He asked me, Why don't you come up and pitch horseshoes? I've been pitching ever since."

The game's a great equalizer. Doctors, truck drivers, engineers, salesmen, submarine builders—they're all teammates. Most players never miss a week. "If you have a demanding schedule, you tell people never to plan anything for Thursday night because it's horseshoe night," admits John.

What's kept this game going so long here? League secretary Rudy Urban thinks it might be "as simple as a man, metal, and dirt sport that provides a welcome release from life's demanding routines."

Recently the league has gone high tech with averages and handicaps totaled by computer. But there's one thing that won't change: If it's summer, and it's Thursday, in Deep River, it's horseshoe night.

THE LURE OF THE WATER

CLOCKWISE FROM TOP LEFT: **TYING A FLY IN CHESTER; KAYAKERS AT THE ANNUAL MILFORD OYSTER FESTIVAL; LAUNCHING FROM A BEACH IN MADISON; CLASSIC WOODEN BOATS IN MYSTIC; LOOKING FOR SEA CREATURES IN WESTBROOK; SAILING OFFSHORE OF WESTPORT.**

Life Is a Cheer of Bowls

Did you know that Bowling Green, Kentucky, and the Tavern on the Green in New York are both named after a sport that is both ancient *and* on the rise here in Connecticut?

It's called lawn bowling, though Italians have a similar game they call bocce. At the Fernleigh Lawn Bowling Club in West Hartford, they play a game that the British brought to the Colonies. Anti-British feeling after the Revolution affected its popularity, but in the mid-1800s lawn bowling made a comeback.

"What we have here is called a green. It's as flat as you can get it," explains the head of the club, Gordon Fowler, walking the length of the playing field.

The object is to roll the bowl (not ball), racking up points by getting closest to the small white ball known as the jack, which may be as much as one hundred feet away. Players use what's called a "biased" bowl. It's lopsided so it curves toward the flat side as it slows down.

"You don't have to be a great athlete to do it reasonably well. That's not to say I do it reasonably well," Gordon demurs. "But on the other hand, it is something that is a lot of fun. And believe it or not, there is a little exercise involved."

Once a men-only club, Fernleigh is now coed. Ellen Boyne is widely thought to be the club's best player of either sex. Ellen also belongs to one of Connecticut's three other lawn bowling clubs, the Thistle Club at Elizabeth Park in Hartford.

"You need a little more time to play golf and you need a little more money to play golf," says Ellen, a big enthusiast. "This is a relatively inexpensive sport. You buy your bowls, and you can buy them used, and all you need is a pair of sneakers."

Some clubs require dress whites, even blazers and ties, but Fernleigh is more relaxed—and recruiting new members. "Once you try it you are hooked," claims Ellen.

Keep On Bugling

They call themselves the Connecticut Alumni Senior Drum and Bugle Corps, and they step off smartly for more than a dozen parades a year, including the Italian Festival in Westport.

For twenty years now the eighty members of the corps have been rehearsing in Seymour, but they drive there from as far away as Stafford Springs and New Milford. They come from all walks of life. They are as young as fourteen and as old as seventy-six, but mostly they're musicians who played in drum corps years ago and didn't want the music to end.

Jim Crowley is a former director of the corps. Like most of the members, he's a veteran of other drum and bugle corps. "Most of it was in high school and college, and then I continued before I went in the service," Jim says.

Mike Preuss, a tool-and-die maker, is a bugler. "In a regular drum corps, it's more intense," he says. "You practically give yourself over every weekend, where this is more laid back and is a casual and fun thing." Competitive corps took too much time away from work and family, so the alumni corps seems to fill the bill. "After I retired from drum corps for a while, a bunch of the guys decided to get together. Once you have it in your blood you never get rid of it," he says with a grin.

Dave Paulis plays the contrabass—the bugle version of a tuba, an instrument he estimates weighs about twenty-five pounds. And is it fun to carry around during a parade? "Oh, it's fantastic!" is his enthusiastic reply.

The corps' musical selections run the gamut from the Hallelujah Chorus from Handel's *Messiah* to the theme from the Steve McQueen movie *The Magnificent Seven*.

Jean Uhelsky, a member of the honor guard, says there's another benefit. "It's given me a chance to see a lot of the state that I had never seen before, because we go coast to coast in state, from New London to Greenwich." Some of the musicians share memories that date back to high school, and now they make new ones in their retirement years. "We used to bum cigarettes, now we bum Polident!" says one, laughing.

There's one bond that keeps the alumni corps together—the smiles and cheers of the spectators as they pass by in formation. And as baritone player Mannie Padin admits, "The underlying thing is the love of music and comradeship."

Chasing Steeples

Biking is big in Connecticut. The summer pastime ranges from international professional team cycling in the Tour of Connecticut Housatonic Valley Classic (with a 120-mile course for the men and 70-mile course for the women), to pedaling your mountain bike through a state forest or cruising down a country lane lined with a cooling canopy of trees.

If you want a combination of exercise and sightseeing, and the good feeling that comes from helping someone else, the Steeple Chase Bike Tour on the third Saturday in August is for you. The hundred-, fifty-, and twenty-mile routes wind through the scenic northeastern corner of Connecticut, passing panoramic views, picturesque farms, and leafy woods. Rest stops are at some of the most historic churches in the region—hence *Steeple Chase*. Cyclists see the Hampton Congregational Church, built in 1754, which is the second oldest Congregational meetinghouse in the state. The United Baptist Church in Westford was built in 1840 with a floor that slopes toward the pulpit. In Lebanon stands the only remaining building designed by the Revolutionary War artist John Trumbull. It dates to 1804.

For a dozen years the ride has been a fund-raiser for two nonprofit social service agencies. Riders are rewarded with a beautiful day in the country, homemade food at all the church rest stops, and a chance to make a difference in someone's life.

Cupid's Arrow

Buck Kalinowski sees potential in both people and horses, even when others can't.

At his Wolcott farm, Hillside Equestrian Meadows, Buck hires people with disabilities, like Matteo Marignani. As a teen Matteo suffered a serious brain injury in a car accident.

"This keeps me moving," Matteo says with a million-dollar smile. "If I wasn't here I'd probably be doing nothing, watching TV, getting a beer belly. This job gives me something to do. Actually it gives me a lot of things to do."

Buck thinks everyone deserves another chance, and that's how he came to find a little brown mare for sale at an auction just after Valentine's Day in 1999. She was very fearful, sick, emaciated, and marked with a perfect heart on her face. The mare was about to be sold by the pound for horsemeat when Buck bid on her.

"No one wanted her, not even for $325," he says, shaking his head. "They led her up and down and this little horse just lifted up her head, let out a whinny, looked at me, and I didn't even think about it—my hand just went like this," he says, raising his hand in the air.

Buck took her home and called her Cupid because of the heart on her face. "Her hips were sticking out, you could count every rib in her body. The vet came here the day we had her delivered and he said, 'I don't want to bust your bubble, but I'd be really surprised if this horse makes it through the night.'"

She did. Buck and his staff nursed Cupid back to health, and she doubled her weight from a sickly three hundred pounds to more than seven hundred. Young visitors from the country and from the inner city loved her and helped her get over her fear of people. She learned to carry riders, won a ribbon at a horse show, and even enjoys a swim in the farm's pond.

But all through those first months at Hillside Cupid had a secret. Buck was away when he got a phone call from the farm. "It's from Gail, who is our trainer. She says 'Buck, Cupid had a baby.' And I'm thinking, 'We have over a hundred horses. Cupid? Cupid wasn't even pregnant.' But Gail responded, "Oh, yes, she was, and this baby has an amazing little arrow on his back."

Buck flew home to see for himself. "I arrived ten o'clock at night. I went down to the barn, flicked on the light, and my lower jaw dropped. That's how amazing it was to see."

And there he was, born against the odds to a mother who wasn't expected to live, Cupid's Arrow.

Ten-year-old Taylor Allen, a regular rider from Wolcott, remembers seeing Arrow for the first time. "I thought it was just amazing! I was just like thunderstruck. I just couldn't believe it."

Since then Cupid and Arrow have become celebrities, and Arrow has turned into a bit of a ham. He loves to do tricks with Buck, including shaking hands and bowing deeply to his adoring fans. Buck has written two kids' books about them, with lessons about never giving up and being yourself. The horses have been immortalized as Breyer's collectibles, as Beanie Babies, on T-shirts and all sorts of paraphernalia. Buck's even writing a screenplay for a movie about the rescued mare and her colt.

"Kids relate to Cupid as the little underdog, the little horse that no one wanted, the little horse that the others made fun of," Buck says. "She learned to trust again and give it another chance and now she's started to get this big circle of friends."

Children who are seriously ill or who have disabilities often write to Cupid and Arrow. "Here's a horse that was ready to be destroyed and her life changed, just because some people took an interest in her and decided to lend her a helping hand," he says. "And I think Arrow was a little gift for all the animals like Cupid that we've worked with here."

And the Livin' Is Easy

I'm fortunate to have married a man who reminds me to take time to smell the roses. How easy it is to forget to do that! Somehow we think their blooms won't fade, that summer will last forever, and the livin' will be easy for months unending. Summer is the season for waking up late, sipping morning coffee on the deck, and donning a T-shirt, flip-flops, and a bathing suit to wear until it's time to put your pajamas back on. It's the time we set aside to tackle a novel while sprawled on the beach. 'Tis the season to turn off the oven, fire up the grill, and gather family and friends for hamburgers, hot dogs, potato salad, and picnic food that's easy to make and goes down easy, too, with a fresh-squeezed lemonade or iced tea in a tall glass, dripping with condensation and topped off with a sprig of mint from the garden.

Take that tea on the front porch and spend hours in a rocking chair, watching the world go by, while you catch up with relatives visiting from out of town. Or make memories that will be pasted into scrapbooks when winter arrives, of family vacations in woodland cabins or seaside bungalows, furnished with a broom to sweep out the sand and a cooler to carry to the beach.

Remember the day as a kid when you took your first dive off the side of the pool, and the dozens of "cannonballs" that splashed all the grown-ups? It still feels good to shriek out loud while speeding down the deepest dip in the country's biggest wooden roller coaster at its oldest amusement park, or to pack up the van and take in the best show in town at one of the last drive-in movie theaters left in the United States.

In summer in Connecticut, you don't have to drive too far to find a place to linger on a lazy afternoon. There are yard sales, tag sales, garage sales, rummage sales at church suppers, library book sales, perfect for browsing or for books to read while swinging in the hammock or to tuck into a beach bag. There are sidewalk art sales, antiques for sale under bright white tents, flea markets in parking lots, and nostalgic cruise nights when high-gloss, hand-buffed, much-beloved vintage cars roll out for the evening.

As a kid I relished the annual opening up and airing out of my grandparents' summer cottage and the chance to see summertime friends who lived far away the rest of the year. Connecticut's campgrounds and marinas are places to make new friends, whether it's the family in the next tent or the people down the pier in their new powerboat. After all, in summertime, the livin' is easy.

The Beacon

Speeding back to the island two miles off shore in Norwalk that he and his children have called home for three months, it's clear David Graaf feels he landed a great summer job.

"I looked at it as an opportunity not only to do something unusual that would live with me for the rest of my life," he says, "but also to get an education about the wildlife and nature of the area."

David is the only full-time live-in lighthouse keeper left on Long Island Sound, though that's using the term loosely, since the Sheffield Island Lighthouse has been dark for more than one hundred years. But the lighthouse and nature preserve are popular tourist attractions maintained by the Norwalk Seaport Association. A former labor negotiator, David has been a stay-at-home dad since his wife's career brought them from South Africa to Stamford. He was wondering what to do with his kids for the summer. "I picked up the newspaper and opened it, and there's an article about Sheffield Island," David says. "It said they were looking for a lighthouse keeper for the summer and so that was that. It leapt

out at me and said, *That's what you need to be doing.*"

David was undeterred to learn that he, Jason, and Caity would live in a 177-year-old cottage, not in the stone lighthouse, a mansion by comparison. The cottage has no running water, no indoor plumbing, very little furniture, and no electricity. "If anything, that was an attraction for me. I thought, Great! Get away and do something completely different. It just seemed like one of those opportunities that comes along once in a lifetime. When it does, *do it!*"

Some kids might have whined about leaving friends and video games behind, but eleven-year-old Jason and nine-year-old Caitlin were enthralled. "I hoped we would do it because it would be a really good experience. And even if we didn't like it, just to try it out and see how it was, just so we know," says Caitlin.

Jason says this summer has been much more productive than one spent hanging around at home. What else would he have done with the school break? "I guess wasted it away watching TV, so I think it's good to be out here," he admits.

"Jason said to me the other day that he loves it out here because he doesn't have any of the other stress that he has at home," his father confides. "Now, I am not sure that an eleven-year-old has major stress living in Stamford, but I think what he was saying was that the environment is just that much more peaceful here."

Peaceful maybe, but it's not lonely. Every few hours a ferry arrives from the seaport and deposits visitors, who marvel at the island's tranquility and beauty. David greets them as they disembark with a few words of advice. "For those of you who want to go up in the lighthouse, I can highly recommend it.

I've done it about two hundred times this summer, so it's well worth the climb."

Some envy the Graafs. Chuck McManus and his wife have toured more than sixty lighthouses since he retired from the navy. Chuck is eyeing the job himself, and says, "If I could bring my dog out here, I would volunteer for next year!" Others like George Reid of Wilton say a two-hour visit and picnic are enough. "It's a lovely spot and it's very much a part of Americana as we know it." But, he adds emphatically, "I could live out here *one day. One!*"

Unlike lighthouse keepers of the past, David Graaf has no beacon to keep watch over. He's busy, though, with chores from hauling rainwater to cleaning tables for evening clambakes to keeping the lawn mowed. And David isn't the only member of the family working on an island. His wife does, too, though not quite as peaceful a one—it's the island of Manhattan. Gillian Graaf works in New York as a business analyst, and the kids go home with David to spend a couple of days a week with her.

"She has always said that it's her ambition to live on an island and be self-sufficient," David says, smiling, when asked what his wife thought of his summer adventure. "So she could hardly argue when the opportunity came up for us to do it."

While giving up the luxuries of modern-day living, David, Jason, and Caity have all gained something over the summer. Jason has a great back-to-school essay to write. "I have a feeling it will be a very long essay. I am just going to say that I had a great time out here—it was great."

Caity has advice for her friends. "I'll tell them they better come and have some fun out here. The ferry's running and they should come, it's really nice out here."

And their father has had a chance to remember what really matters. "We get into situations in everyday life where we get wrapped up in problems that seem at times insurmountable. We start looking for obstacles in our lives. Whereas I think that life was intended to be a whole lot more simple," he reflects. "You need this kind of experience on a regular basis to keep going in the right direction and your perspective on life correct."

The Sheffield Island beacon that once guided ships is long gone. But for the Graaf family, it seems the light is still shining.

WATERFRONT LIVING

CLOCKWISE FROM TOP LEFT: SWINGING IN STONY CREEK; GUILFORD TOWN DOCK; LAKESIDE IN LEBANON; DOCKSIDE IN ESSEX; PENSIVE MOMENTS IN STONY CREEK. FACING PAGE: THE MOON RISES OVER BARRIER SANDBARS AT THE CONNECTICUT AUDUBON COASTAL CENTER IN MILFORD.

Connecticut River Museum

Basie the Book Boy

Summertime is ripe for reading on the beach, or in a hammock under a tree, and for hunting for books at tag sales, library sales, and secondhand bookstores. Most kids end school with a summer reading list, and that's never a problem for one North Branford teen.

It's rare to see fifteen-year-old Basie Gitlin without a book. Not just when he's on campus at Choate Rosemary Hall, and not just when he's in class. At Basie's house in North Branford, he's surrounded by books, used books. The Gitlin household boasts more books than some public libraries—about fifteen thousand volumes. "I believe every room in the house has books in it," says Basie, "including both bathrooms and the kitchen and obviously the living room."

Basie comes by his interest in books naturally. His dad, Jay, is a historian at Yale. His mom, Ginny Bales, says for her husband, "It's like an occupational hazard." Jay chimes in: "You go to the offices

of most history professors and the walls are just bursting with books."

Ginny, a former college professor, loves to read, but says Basie inherited the "collector gene" from Dad. Does she ever meet them at the door and say, "Not one more book in this house"? With a wide smile, Ginny says, "I've discovered it is completely futile. I just keep saying to myself there are so many things they could be into that could be so much worse. They're into things that make them smart and interesting to talk to, and the books themselves are really great. It's just that I would like to have a more normal house and to have a space that wasn't so dominated by books."

Bookshelves line every wall, and divide some rooms in sections. There are stacks and stacks of books neatly organized and piled on the furniture, on kitchen counters, and on shelves in the bathrooms and the basement.

Basie's collection is eclectic, but focused. He has entire series of some children's storybooks, and then, "since my dad teaches social history, I've looked out for books for children that address similar things as his books do that are more scholarly. For instance, he might have a book on the making of glass and I have one that outlines the same principles and steps."

Basie can put his hands on any volume in minutes. "My memory isn't that great for most things," he claims, "but then for books I can usually remember when I got it, where I got it, and how much I paid for it. If it's ex-library, what library it belonged to in the past."

Although they take an empty suitcase on every

vacation to fill with newly discovered books, Jay and Basie can often be found roaming through second-hand bookstores all over the state. One of their favorites is Whitlock Farm Booksellers in Bethany.

"Basie's always been able to classify things and been very intrigued by older things," says Jay. "This was his way into the past. People who loved old cars, who loved old records, who loved old books really latched on to him from an early age. It's like, 'Here's a kid who gets it.' They were so pleased always to meet a child like this."

Basie and Jay agree that Connecticut is a great place to unearth used books, because the people who live here have varied and interesting tastes. "I think the number one thing is the thrill of the hunt," says Basie. "Some people will use Internet sites to find the books they're looking for. But that doesn't work all that well for me, because I look for things that I don't know exist yet. So I have no idea what I'm going to find until I find it. Really, I'm a true browser."

With a son named after Count Basie, you might have guessed that this family has another passion—making music. Their band plays nearly every weekend. They even have their own theme song.

In an alcove surrounded by books, with Jay at the piano and Basie on drums, Ginny sings to the tune of "You've Got to Have Heart" from *Damn Yankees*: "You've got to have books, lots and lots and lots of books. Doesn't matter if you've read them yourself, as long as they look good on the shelf. You've got to have tomes full of histories or poems. You may think you have enough books to read, there's always one more you really need."

Will Basie start yet another collection? "Well," he says, "if I were to develop another interest, it could become possibly more important. But I would never really lose the books."

THE JOYS OF SUMMER

CLOCKWISE FROM TOP LEFT: ROCKING CHAIRS BECKON IN OLD SAYBROOK; RIVER-FEST FIREWORKS OVER THE CONNECTICUT RIVER AT HARTFORD; LILIES ALONGSIDE A SEAFRONT COTTAGE IN NOANK; POLISHING UP SUMMER READING ON A PORCH IN GROTON.

The Simple Life

Ask ten-year-old triplets Laura, Crystal, and Monique Bellemare what they like about camping at Hammonasset Beach State Park and they shout in unison, "Everything but the mosquitoes."

Then they happily start counting their bug bites, which they estimate at "ten million, at least." If you think an occasional mosquito is the biggest challenge in taking the Waterbury triplets and their three-year-old brother, Roy, camping, ask their grandmother Elizabeth Winnie, who is making breakfast over a charcoal grill.

"I am trying to make toast but it's not working too well," Elizabeth points out. "I told the kids this is roughing it. It takes a long time but you'll get toast—*some*day!"

The kids are camping in tents for a week with their dad, Roy Salerno, their aunt Maryann LeBel, and their grandparents. "We have a double dome tent with a tunnel connecting them—the women sleep on one side, the kids in the other," Maryann explains. There's a separate tent for the men, and another for supplies.

"It's hectic with four kids, trying to get them settled the first day—that's hard," Roy says. "Then they get their routine going. They like to take a bike ride before breakfast, and soon the hardest thing is getting them back here to eat."

"We've done it since they were infants," says Maryann. "This is easier than when they were babies with playpens and all that. We love Hammonasset—it's so clean, and they offer activities for the kids, though we make our own activities, too. I did this with my son and he's twenty-one now. We spent days collecting seashells and rocks and pinecones. Got to keep the kids occupied."

And they are occupied, making crafts, fishing and crabbing with their dad and grandfather, riding bikes, and preparing their next performance for the campers who attend the outdoor movie night. Laura is considering reciting the Gettysburg Address, and

with a little encouragement from her sisters, she launches into it, while the other two shout, "Hey, don't forget the hand movements."

Meanwhile, just a few campsites away, the Jordan family is packing up after three weeks at Hammonasset. "We like having a fire at night, and making s'mores, of course," says Mark Jordan. "After I step in hot marshmallows a few times I wonder if we really should keep making them, but . . ."

Mark and Stephanie Jordan live with their three daughters in Meriden, close enough so they commute daily to work and camp in the evenings and on weekends. "It's only a forty-minute drive, but you feel like you are thousands of miles from home!" says Stephanie. Still, it's close enough that she can drive to her second job, as a member of an auto racing team, which is on the circuit all summer.

The Jordans camp in their Dutchmen travel trailer, which they tow behind a Chevy Tahoe. Although the campground has no hookups for sewer, septic, or power, they get by on their camper's generator. Stephanie likes getting the kids away from the trappings of home.

Fourteen-year-old Jessica has been working on her backstroke at the beach just beyond the campground, hoping to make her high school swim team in the fall. And while eight-year-old Mikayla got to know almost everyone in camp, five-year-old Sara learned to ride her bike without the training wheels. "The girls all play sports, so August is our month for family time—that's why we come here," Mark says. "It's about the only time none of us are busy."

Hammonasset campers mingle and wave, including people "roughing it" in pup tents and sleeping bags, all the way up to the motor coach that Holly Roy's teenage nephew mistook for a rock star's bus when he saw it the first time. Holly and her husband, Norm, plan to sell their house in Suffield in a couple of years and travel full time in their forty-foot-long Holiday Rambler Endeavor. They're camped next to a similar coach owned by Holly's aunt and uncle, Pat and Ron Gronback from Wethersfield. If your idea of camping is a hotel without room service, you might want to try this.

"I fell in love with this coach," says Holly, and it's easy to see why. Martha Stewart designed the interior, with cherrywood cabinets and paneling. You'll

also find draperies with coordinated valances, tapestry fabrics, tasseled pillows, a double refrigerator, freezer and icemaker with cherry-paneled doors, a convection oven, a microwave and conventional oven, two TVs, and windows with awnings big enough to cover an entire picnic table and extra chairs for guests. There's Internet access via cell phone, even a fax machine. At night the two families use the kitchenette to cook meals like shrimp scampi or beef roasted in wine.

Both couples love Hammonasset for its beach, biking, and birding. Although there are 550 campsites, Pat notes, "It's really pretty quiet, even though there are lots of families and kids here."

Although they may be traveling in style, Holly admits that with her Hobie catamaran on the roof, the bikes attached to the back, and towing a jeep, "my son-in-law says we look like the Clampetts of the *Beverly Hillbillies* coming down the road!" Still, she insists, this is the way to go. "There are so many beautiful places in this country. Flying is great, but you miss all the beauty."

Best Show in Town

"Come on down for the best show in town, the Mansfield Drive-In"—the jingle blasts from speakers set up around the parking lot.

You don't hear many ads for drive-ins anymore, because there aren't many left.

"The first time I came and saw this place, it looked like a place that nobody loved, but it was really a beautiful piece of property," says ponytailed owner Michael Jungden with a gleam in his eye. When Michael took over the Mansfield theater in the early 1970s, drive-in movie theaters all over the country were already becoming a thing of the past, thanks to rising land values and then, later, to the popularity of cable TV and VCRs.

"I just thought that there was a way to make it work, that I could make something happen," says Michael. "I was also thinking about the fact that someday I'd be the only one doing this."

He nearly is—his is one of two active drive-ins left in Connecticut. Michael took a chance and added two *more* screens to the original one at the time most other drive-ins were going dark. "It just so happened that the year that I put up the new screens they ran the cable for cable TV in town, so that took a bite out of me," he says, shaking his head.

But his determination paid off. On a recent summer evening, cars from as far away as New Haven and even out of state lined up well before dark. Fran Burba, who collects admission, remarks: "I've had customers all the way from Hawaii, Guatemala, Alaska, you name it."

In spring and early fall the drive-in is open Friday, Saturday, and Sunday, but in peak season—summer—it's open seven nights a week. Despite its remote location, the Mansfield Drive-In packs them in—up to a thousand cars a night. During the midweek special admission is fourteen bucks, no matter how many people are in the car, and they see a double feature of two first-run movies. It's a deal some families can't pass up, especially when they pack all the comforts of home.

Christine Parr and her two sisters have outfitted their minivan roof with an air mattress, some baby bed rails, and a cooler full of snacks. She laughs and explains, "We very rarely get to go out all together with no kids and no husbands and stuff, so it's kind of like a girls' night out. And we get to binge!" Twenty-five years ago

Coreen Margnelli came here with her boyfriend; now she brings her kids. "They like to come in their pajamas 'cause it gets kind of late on the ride home. We have chairs, we bring a radio, so sitting out we can hear the movie."

Maritca Candelario and her kids are perched on the hood of their Camaro. "I like it better because there's more space and fresh air," she says.

Michael agrees that at a drive-in the rules are relaxed, and so is the atmosphere. "You go into an indoor theater and everybody has to hush to watch the movie. Whereas at a drive-in, they sit in the car, they can talk to each other, they can bring their kids. If their kids are unruly, they can deal with their kids without having to disturb the rest of the crowd."

Jamie Langevin comes from South Windsor because "you can get up, you can walk around, and you can do whatever you want. The kids love it because they can walk around." And people do, hopping from car to car, visiting friends and neighbors.

In the heyday of Connecticut drive-ins, there were some forty across the state. Across the nation the number of drive-ins peaked at more than four thousand. Today there are just over four hundred nationwide. One secret to Michael's success: "I do everything. I repair things, I'm the projection booth repairman, and I'm the soda machine repairman. When the soda machine breaks I fix it because by the time Pepsi gets here I've already lost a few hundred dollars."

Before buying the drive-in, Michael sold auto parts, a job that wasn't nearly as much fun. "Nobody comes to see you when they're happy—they already have a broken car. Whereas here, in this business, everybody comes in, they're in a great mood."

A Connecticut summer, a drive-in movie—who could blame them?

Thrills, Chills, and Old-fashioned Fun

Forget Coney Island. If it's steamy and sunny and you're hankering for a break, pack up the kids and come to one of Connecticut's own homegrown amusement parks for a dose of both history and fun.

The nation's oldest amusement park is found right here in Bristol. In 1846 **Lake Compounce** opened as a "picnic park." Proprietor Gad Norton offered public swimming and rowing as well as band concerts in a gazebo on shore. The Casino, the first permanent building on the site, opened in 1895 as a restaurant and ballroom. In 1911 visitors enjoyed their first whirls on a carousel that is still operating. Three years later the Green Dragon, the park's first electric-powered roller coaster, thrilled riders. The cost to ride it was one thin dime. The Wildcat replaced it in 1927, and has become a classic. (On its seventy-fifth anniversary, Noel Abue, a Meriden

postal worker, broke his own record for consecutive rides on the Wildcat when he hit 2,002!)

In the late 1920s speedboats made waves on the lake. The ballroom was expanded and dancers enjoyed the sounds of the big bands including Cab Calloway, Count Basie, and Benny Goodman. In 1941 five thousand dancers set an all-time record for attendance at the ballroom when a young singer named Frank Sinatra appeared there with the

Tommy Dorsey orchestra. In that same era the Norton family and its partners purchased the miniature steam railroad that had been the creation of William Gillette, and the train encircled the lake until recently, when the park returned it to Gillette Castle, its original home.

Six generations of the Norton family owned and operated Lake Compounce until 1985, and for decades it was also the site of a summertime political institution known as the Crocodile Club. Today Lake Compounce is owned by the Kennywood Entertainment Company. Compounce spokesman Richard Bisi says Kennywood liked Lake Compounce because of its lovely setting and saw that "it was not a cookie-cutter park." Since 1997 they have spent fifty million dollars at the park, adding new attractions like Boulder Dash, voted the world's number one wooden coaster by the National Amusement Park Historical Association, and a water park that includes a partially enclosed raft ride known as Mammoth Falls as well as Clipper Cove, a tall ship that douses bathers with buckets of water to their shrieking delight.

Quassy Amusement Park, on the shore of Lake Quassapaug in Middlebury, opened in 1908 as a "trolley park"—these were often built by the trolley companies at the end of their lines to encourage more passengers to ride the rails. At one time there were nearly a thousand trolley parks in America; now Quassy is one of only eleven left, and of course the trolley that once brought visitors here is long gone. Still, the spring-fed lake continues to offer swimming, and there are more than two dozen rides on Quassy's twenty acres. Some of the newer ones are the Frog Hopper, The Big Flush Water Coaster, and Saturation Station, a family water play area at the beach.

Quassy has a long history of carousels, including one that nearly went up in flames after a business dispute with new owners in 1937. The animals were saved and the carousel reassembled. That carousel ran until 1989 when maintenance costs forced the park to sell it, and on its last day long lines formed of people who wanted one more ride on the merry-go-round. A new carousel opened the following year, but the oldest ride in the park is the Kiddie Carousel, built in 1924 at that *other* amusement park, Coney Island.

DREAMING OF ENDLESS SUMMER AT THE BEACH

CLOCKWISE FROM TOP: HAMMONASSET BEACH STATE PARK, MADISON; SPRITE ISLAND, NORWALK; JOIE DE VIVRE IN MADISON; THE PERFECT YELLOW TUBE, CLINTON; A HORSESHOE CRAB FROM NORWALK'S TIDAL INLETS.

Lemonade Stands across America

You might think Jack Tregenza, at only seven years old, is a little young to be an entrepreneur or philanthropist. But the truth is, he's both. When Jack was about four years old, he saw a story on TV about children suffering in war-torn Kosovo. He wanted to help. So with some assistance from his mom, Robin, Jack sold lemonade at the Rowayton Memorial Day parade and donated the proceeds to charities that help kids in troubled places—charities like Stamford's Americares, which has provided disaster and humanitarian relief to 137 nations worldwide. The first year Jack, his little brother Charlie, and his friend Tripp Lawghon raised thirty-eight dollars, but they have raised as much as six hundred selling lemonade, cookies, and cupcakes.

Today Jack's lemonade stand sports a sign that reads LEMONADE STANDS ACROSS AMERICA, ALL PROCEEDS TO AMERICARES. Jack's good idea is spreading, and family friends have adopted it, opening Memorial Day parade lemonade stands for Americares in Darien and elsewhere in Norwalk, as well as in faraway towns in Colorado, North Carolina, and upstate New York. Jack understands that soldiers aren't the only ones who can fight for freedom; kids can help, too.

Cruising

The way Ruth and Don Jack see it, the 1953 Agate Red Oldsmobile Holiday was meant to come into their lives.

After all, they had a car *just* like it when they were dating (though Ruth recalls that that one was a convertible). She still seems a little wistful about trading it in for a 1956 Pontiac when they got married. Over the last few years, the Jacks hunted everywhere for a car like the one they had as young lovers.

They traveled all over to car shows, even flying to Texas, scanned all the trade magazines and papers without finding one. Then one day, according to Ruth, "A friend of ours drove by, and he says, 'You know of anyone who wants a '53 Olds?' He knew of one only ten miles away in a barn."

But when they went to see it, it was in rough shape. "There was a gas can in the front seat with a hose to the carburetor to start it, and you couldn't see out the windows they were so dirty." Ruth shakes her head. "So I go back to our truck and say 'Don, you come when you're through.' The owner

says to him, 'Take it around the property but be careful, it has no brakes.'"

Don didn't buy the Olds, but a few weeks later he went, cash in hand, to look at a Model A, and decided not to buy that one, either.

"The next day I go grocery shopping," Ruth says, "and I get back and there's my husband, son, and daughter-in-law with big grins on their faces. There's the '53 Olds from the barn in my driveway."

Turned out Ruth and this particular car went way back, too. "When we looked at the paperwork, we found out the car's original owner lived two houses away from the house where I grew up with my parents!"

So you can understand if Ruth seems just a little proud as visitors stop to give the completely restored red Olds a long look at the weekly Northeast Cruisers car show at the Blue Sky Diner in Stratford. These shows go on just about every night of the week somewhere in Connecticut in good weather, generally accompanied by oldies tunes and enthusiastic car collectors and lookers of all ages.

Cliff Haslam, a painting contractor from Stratford, is buffing his '59 Chevy Impala four-door sedan. He says, "I love '59 Chevies. I love everything about them, the fins, the dashboard, the taillights, the interior, the steering wheel, the colors—everything!"

Cliff says the extreme cat's-eye taillights are just part of what he loves about that model year. "If you look at '59s across the board they are all radical, I don't care if it's Chrysler or Olds or whatever. " But he admits that some of his car buff friends disagree. "I have friends who say, 'Four doors is two doors too many, Cliff, not cool.' But I don't care—if it's a '59 it could be a station wagon and I'd love it!"

Other car collectors pull in. Eighty-eight-year-old Ken Stebbins arrives in a bright red 1952 Jaguar XK 120. It gleams with chrome and oozes class. It's hard to imagine that at one time it raced at Lime Rock. Ken frequents these cruise nights because "it's a lot of effort, time and expenditure to get a car to this point, and how else are you going to realize what you've done? People look at it, they admire it, and they like it. They want to sit in it, and that's the enjoyment you get out of it." Of course, driving it is another thing! "My neighbors feel I am a crazy old guy driving a Jaguar, so I am looked at as kind of a character in Stratford, you know," he admits with a note of pride in his voice. "I also own a 1942 Packard convertible, which is a show car. I drive that when I feel my age. When I feel eighteen I get into this."

The music, the shiny vintage autos, the friendly folks—they all attract a crowd, even some who didn't think they really cared much about cars. "This car turns heads for sure," Cliff Haslam explains. "When I turn the radio on and start to cruise with it, people are enjoying it along with me. I got in back of a guy in a pickup tonight and he heard my cassette blaring and he was just looking in the mirror and grinning."

Acknowledgments

As you may have guessed from reading this book, summer is my favorite time of year in Connecticut. The season energizes us for the bracing New England winters to come. This book is an attempt to capture the glow of summer sunbeams, and it happened because of many people.

To Paula Brisco, who gave up hours of gardening once coaxed out of her publishing hiatus, there are not enough ways to say thank you. Besides being a wonderful and caring editor, your "good vibes" bolstered my spirits even when rain or chill threatened parades and picnics. To the team at Globe Pequot Press: It is a joy to work with you. Nancy Freeborn's layouts bring summer to life, and Sue Preneta waded through thousands of photos to find these gems. Thanks also to Jane Reilly, Laura Strom, Liz Taylor, Laura Jorstad, and of course the indefatigable Larry Dorfman.

Thank you to the photographers who found smiles, excitement, and moments of contemplative beauty that others might have overlooked.

I cannot express enough gratitude to my producer, researcher, sounding board and, most of all, dear friend Michele Russo. She shows her devotion daily in more ways than can be counted.

CPTV is my home for telling many of these *Positively Connecticut* stories, and I thank Jerry Franklin and Jay Whitsett for that. To the show's sponsors, John Klein of People's Bank, and Arthur Diedrick, the chairman of the Connecticut Development Authority, thank you for believing that sharing the good news about Connecticut is critical. Bette Blackwell, you make the TV stories better than they are in my imagination, and your talent for titles is unsurpassed. Ed Gonsalves, thanks for always making it happen, somehow. Joan Gurski and Judy Pansullo, thanks for your deft field producing on two of my favorites.

To Ray Dunaway and my other colleagues at WTIC NewsTalk 1080, thanks for understanding the demands of deadlines.

To the people within these pages who shared their lives and their stories, you motivate all of us to care more about Connecticut.

In memory of my grandmother, who lived to be eighty-seven, sustained by her delight in summer's unique pleasures, and in honor of my parents, who transformed their teenage "summer love" into a fifty-year marriage, thanks for the inspiration.

To my husband, Tom, who reminds me to smell the roses and marvel at sunsets, and who spent the summer seeking one more great shot of our favorite lighthouse, thanks for your love, patience, and endurance.

Resources

Fresh Flavors

The Sweet Life, page 2: Rose's Berry Farm, 295 Matson Hill Road, South Glastonbury; (860) 633–7467; www.rosesberryfarm.com.

Strawberry Shortcake and Cream, page 4: Rowayton United Methodist Church, 5 Pennoyer Street, Norwalk; (203) 838-0049.

The Best of the Wurst, page 5: Jane and Michael Stern, www.roadfood.com. Super Duper Weenie, 306 Black Rock Turnpike, Fairfield; (203) 334–DOGS; www.superduperweenie.com. Blackie's, 2200 Waterbury Road, Cheshire; (203) 699–1819. Swanky Franks, 182 Connecticut Avenue (exit 14 off I–95), Norwalk; (203) 838–8969. Funki Munki, Chapel Street, New Haven; www.funkimunki.com. Doogie's, 2525 Berlin Turnpike, Newington; (860) 666–6200. Rawley's Drive-In, 1886 Post Road, Fairfield; (203) 259–9023.

New Haven's Frostiest, page 8: New Haven Colony Historical Society, 114 Whitney Avenue, New Haven; (203) 562–4183.

I Scream, You Scream, We All Scream, page 9: Dr. Mike's, 158 Greenwood Avenue, Bethel; (203) 792–4388; 444 Main Street, Monroe; (203) 452–0499. Tulmeadow Farm, 255 Farms Village Road (Route 309), West Simsbury; (860) 658–1430. UConn Dairy Bar, 3636 Horsebarn Road Extension, Storrs; (860) 486-2634. Old Lyme Ice Cream Shoppe, 34 Lyme Street, Old Lyme; (860) 434–6942.

Shellfish Tales, page 12: *The Compleat Clammer,* by Christopher Reaske, available from Burford Books Inc., P.O. Box 388, Short Hills, NJ 07078; www.burfordbooks.com. Connecticut Department of Environmental Protection, 79 Elm Street, Hartford; http://dep.state.ct.us. Hillard Bloom Shellfish Inc., 132 Water Street, South Norwalk; (203) 853–1148; www.hillardbloomshellfish.com.

A Taste of Summer, page 16: Old Lyme Mid-Summer Festival, contact www.flogris.org. Cato Corner Cheese, Cato Corner Road, Colchester; (860) 537–3884; catocornerfarm@mindspring.com. Fabled Foods Artisan Breads, call for retail locations: (860) 526–2666.

Falls Brook Organic Farm, 116 Sterling City Road, Lyme; (860) 434–4324. Four Mile River Farm, 124 Four Mile River Road, Old Lyme; (860) 434–2378. Maple Lane Farms, 57 Northwest Corner Road, Preston (860) 889–3766; www.maplelane.com. Sankow's Beaver Brook Farm, 139 Beaver Brook Farm Road, Lyme; (800) 501–WOOL; www.beaverbrookfarm.com. Three Sisters Farm, 11 Evans Lane, Essex; (860) 767–2866.

An Urban Oasis, page 19: Urban Oaks Organic Farm, 225 Oak Street, New Britain; (860) 223–6200.

Arts and Craftspeople

Art and Soul, page 26: For information about Neighborhood Studios, contact the Greater Hartford Arts Council, (860) 525–8629; www.connectthedots.org. For more information on Ed Johnetta Miller, visit www.edjohnetta.com.

En Plein Air, page 28: Connecticut Pastel Society: contact Dick McEvoy in Newtown at (203) 426–8308, or Ralph Schwartz in Monroe at (203) 268–4757.

Hometown Boy, page 30: Monte Cristo Cottage, 325 Pequot Avenue, New London; (860) 443–0051. Eugene

O'Neill Memorial Theater Center, 305 Great Neck Road, Waterford; (860) 443–5378 (box office during summer conferences); www.oneilltheatercenter.org; public performances from early June into August.

A Paradise for Poetry, page 32: Hill-Stead Museum Sunken Garden Poetry Festival, 35 Mountain Road, Farmington; (860) 677–4787; www.Hillstead.org.

Strawhat and Beyond, page 33: The Ivoryton Playhouse Foundation, P.O. Box 458, Ivoryton 06442; (860) 767–7318; www.ivorytonplayhouse.com. Oakdale Theater, 95 South Turnpike Road, Wallingford; (203) 265–1501; www.oakdale.com. The Elm Shakespeare Company, P.O. Box 206029, New Haven 06520; (203) 772–1474; www.elmshakespeare.org (internships go on through summer, performances generally are in August). Westport Country Playhouse, P.O. Box 629, Westport 06881; (203) 227–4177; www.westportplay house.org.

Little Divas, page 36: For information about Take Center Stage, call the Salvation Army at (860) 543–8413. To become a sponsor, contact Connecticut Opera at (860) 527–0713 or www.ctopera.org.

Tanglewood in Connecticut, page 38: Talcott Mountain Music Festival, Iron Horse Boulevard, Simsbury; www.hartfordsymphony.org/talcottmountain.htm. For tickets call HSO Ticket Services at (860) 244–2999, 9:00 A.M. to 5:00 P.M., or call or visit Tickets.com: (800) 447–6849.

Isle of Inspiration, page 40: St. Edmund's Retreat, P.O. Box 399, Enders Island, Mystic 06255; (860) 536–0565; www.endersisland.com.

Family Fare

I Love a Parade, page 46: Barnum Festival: (866) 867–8495 or (203) 367–8495; www.barnumfestival.com. For more information about the Boom Box Parade, call Wayne Norman at (860) 456–1111 or Tara Risley at the Windham Recreation Department, (860) 465–3046. Or visit www.wili.com/am/boombox.htm.

Gillette's Legacy, page 49: Gillette Castle State Park, 67 River Road, East Haddam; (860) 526–2336. River Rep at Ivoryton Playhouse, 103 Main Street, Ivoryton; (860) 767–8348; www.riverrep.com.

Boundless Playgrounds, page 52: Connecticut has twenty-one boundless playgrounds. For information, visit www.boundlessplaygrounds.org or contact the National Center for Boundless Playgrounds, 45 Wintonbury Avenue, Bloomfield 06002; (860) 243–8315.

Painted Ponies, page 55: The New England Carousel Museum, 95 Riverside Avenue (Route 72), Bristol; (860) 585–5411; www.thecarouselmuseum.com. The brochure *Magnificent Carousels of Connecticut* is available at Connecticut Welcome Centers, the New England Carousel Museum, or by calling (800) CT–BOUND. Bushnell Park Carousel, Trinity and Elm Streets, Hartford; (860) 585–5411. Friends of Lighthouse Park Carousel, Box 8531, New Haven, CT 06531.

A Fair to Remember, page 57: For more information and a schedule of state fairs, contact www.ctfairs.org, or write to Association of Connecticut Fairs, Box 563, Somers, CT 06071.

Museums of Trucks and Time, page 60: The Golden Age of Trucking Museum, 1101 Southford Road, Middlebury; (203) 577–2181; www.goldenagetruck museum.com. Timexpo, 175 Union Street, Waterbury; (203) 755–3807; www.timexpo.com.

Amaizing Mazes, page 63: Connecticut aMaizeing Maze, Eddinger Farm, Chamberlain Road, Middletown; (860) 346–3360; www.ctmaze.com. Foster Family Farm, 90 Foster Street, South Windsor; (860) 648–9366; www.fosterfarm.com. Larson's Family Farm, 1055 Federal Road (Route 7), Brookfield; (203) 740–2790; www.larsonsfarmmarket.com. Lyman Orchards, Junction of Routes 147 and 157, Middlefield; (860) 349–1793; www.lymanorchards.com. Plasko's Farm, 670 Daniels Farm Road, Trumbull; (203) 268–2716; www.plaskosfarm.com.

History Alive

Something Old, Something New, page 66: Old New-Gate Prison and Copper Mine, 115 Newgate Road, East Granby; (860) 653–3563; www.chc.state.ct.us/old_new.htm.

Ferry Land, page 69: Connecticut ferries: (860) 443–3856. The Bridgeport/Port Jefferson Steamship Co.: (888) 44–FERRY.

This Thing Called Freedom, page 71: Connecticut State Library and the Museum of Connecticut History, 231 Capitol Avenue, Hartford; (860) 757–6500; www.cslib.org.

A Brave Revenge, page 74: For information about Connecticut Outdoor Drama, Inc., contact David Holdridge at (860) 917–9614 or visit www.benedict arnold.net.

Deep History, page 76: Historic Ship Nautilus and Submarine Force Museum, Naval Submarine Base, 1 Crystal Lake Road, Groton; (800) 343–0079; www.uss nautilus.org.

Bravery and Bagpipes, page 77: Manchester Regional Police and Fire Pipe Band, 39 Daly Road, East Hampton; (860) 267–0903; www.mrpf.net.

Amazing Airmen, page 79: The New England Air Museum, Bradley International Airport, Windsor Locks; (860) 623–3305; www.neam.org.

Schemitzun, page 81: The festival generally takes place in late August on a farm in North Stonington. Call (800) FOXWOODS or visit www.schemitzun.com.

The Blessing of the Fleet, page 82: For information, go to www.ctbound.org or call (800) CT–BOUND.

Natural Wonders

By Any Other Name, page 86: Elizabeth Park, corner of Prospect Avenue and Asylum Avenue, Hartford and West Hartford. Friends of Elizabeth Park, P.O. Box 370361,West Hartford 06137; (860) 231–9443; www.elizabethpark.org.

Seeds of Hope, page 90: Since 1976, the town of Farmington has rented more than two hundred individual garden plots at Kolp Community Gardens on Meadow Road. Sign-up for the plots is held at the Town Hall Council Chambers early in spring on a first-come, first-served basis. For more information, contact the town manager's office: (860) 675–2350.

The Basis of Life, page 92: Comstock, Ferre & Co., 263 Main Street, Wethersfield; (860) 571–6590; www. comstockferre.com. New England Seed Company; (800) 783–7891; www.neseed.com.

We Are the Champions, page 94: The Connecticut College Arboretum, 270 Mohegan Avenue, Box 5201, Connecticut College, New London 06320; (860) 439–5020; http://notabletrees.conncoll.edu. The Bartlett Arboretum, 151 Brookdale Road, North Stamford, is known as the Home of Champions because there are nine notable trees on its property; http://bartlett. arboretum.uconn.edu. Visit www.ct.gov; look up Connecticut Symbols for more on the Charter Oak.

The Black Dog of Meriden, page 97: Hubbard Park, 1 Cahill Avenue, off West Main Street, Meriden; www.cityofmeriden.org. *Legendary Connecticut* by David E. Philips (Willimantic, Conn.: Curbstone Press, 1992); www.curbstone.org.

Star Power, page 98: The John J. McCarthy Observatory is open on almost any clear night after dark. It can also be open in daytime for solar viewing. The observatory is located on the southwest corner of the New Milford High School property, on U.S. Route 7. Schedule a visit by writing, calling, or visiting the Web site: P.O. Box 1144, New Milford 06776; (860) 354–1595; www.mccarthyobservatory.org.

Creatures from the Deep, page 100: Maritime Aquarium, 10 North Water Street, Norwalk; (203) 852–0700; www.maritimeaquarium.org.

A Reverence for Stone, page 104: The Stonewall Initiative: http://stonewall.uconn.edu. Robert Thorson, *Stone by Stone: The Magnificent History in New England's Stone Walls* (New York: Walker & Co., 2002). To contact Professor Thorson, write to SWI, P.O. Box 44, Mansfield 06268-0044, or e-mail robert.thorson@ uconn.edu.

Fields of Dreams, page 106: Blue Slope Country Museum, Inc., 138 Blue Hill Road, Franklin; (860) 642–6413; www.blueslope.com. For information on other farms to visit or for farm maps, contact the Connecticut Department of Agriculture, 765 Asylum Avenue, Hartford 06105; (860) 713–2503; www.state.ct.us/doag.

Let's Play

The Boys of Summer, page 110: Greg Martin, President, Vintage Base Ball Factory, Hartford; (800) 730–8119 or (860) 728–0820; www.vbbf.com.

The Sailor's Life for Me, page 114: Captain John's Sport Fishing Center, 15 First Street, Waterford; (860) 443–7259; www.sunbeamfleet.com. Mystic Whaler Cruises, P.O. Box 189, Mystic 06355; (800) 697–8420 or (860) 536–4218; www.mysticwhaler.com. Maritime Aquarium, 10 North Water Street, Norwalk; (203) 852–0700; www.maritimeaquarium.org. Project Oceanology, 1084 Shennecossett Road, Avery Point, Groton; (800) 364–8472; www.oceanology.org. Sail

Connecticut Access Program, c/o Spectrum Engineering Group, 1111 South Main Street, Cheshire; (203) 294–1524; www.sailctaccess.org. Schooner Sound Learning, 60 South Water Street, New Haven; (203) 865–1737; www.schoonersoundlearning.org. Sound-Waters Schooner, Cove Island Park, 1281 Cove Road, Stamford; (203) 323–1978; www.soundwaters.org.

America's Volunteer Lifesavers, page 117: Visit www.uscgaux.org and enter your zip code to find Coast Guard Auxiliaries near you. They are numerous in Connecticut.

Up and Away, page 118: The Plainville Balloon Festival is usually held the third weekend in August; visit www.plainvilleballoonfestival.com for schedules. Contact Berkshire Balloons at P.O. Box 706, Southington 06489; (203) 250–8441. To find other balloon companies, go to www.ctbound.org or call (800) CT–BOUND.

It's a Ringer, page 120: Deep River Horseshoe League (late April through Labor Day), (860) 526–3517; http://rurban7.home.comcast.net.

Life Is a Cheer of Bowls, page 122: Fernleigh Lawn Bowling Club, Lancaster Road, West Hartford; (860) 232–1040.

Keep on Bugling, page 124: Connecticut Alumni Senior Drum and Bugle Corps, P.O. 781, Shelton 06484; www.ctalumni.org.

Chasing Steeples, page 125: Steeple Chase Bike Tour, P.O. Box 407, Willimantic 06226; (860) 450–7122; www.perceptionprograms.org/tour.htm. Housatonic Valley Classic/Tour of Connecticut, Housatonic Valley Tourism District, 30 Main Street, Danbury; (800) 841–4488 or (203) 743–0546; www.housatonic.org/bike race.htm. For information about other places to pedal, go to www.ctbound.org or call (800) CT–BOUND.

Cupid's Arrow, page 126: Hillside Equestrian Meadows, 1260 Woodtick Road, Wolcott; (203) 879–4631; www.hillsideequestrian.com.

And the Livin' Is Easy

The Beacon, page 130: Norwalk Seaport Association, 132 Water Street, South Norwalk 06854; (203) 838–9444; www.seaport.org.

The Simple Life, page 137: Connecticut offers camping in thirteen state parks or forests. For details, visit http://dep.state.ct.us/stateparks/camping/camping.htm, call (860) 424–3200 or (866) 287–2757, or e-mail dep.stateparks@po.state.ct.us. For information on Connecticut's many privately owned campgrounds, visit www.ctbound.org or call (800) CT–BOUND.

Best Show in Town, page 140: Mansfield Drive-In Theatre, at the junction of Routes 31 and 32 in Mansfield; (860) 423–4441; www.mansfielddrivein.com. Pleasant Valley Drive-In, Route 181 off Route 44 between New Hartford and Barkhamsted, (860) 379–6102.

Thrills, Chills, and Old-fashioned Fun, page 142: Lake Compounce, 822 Lake Avenue, Bristol; (860) 583–3300; www.lakecompounce.com. Lake Quassapaug, Route 64, Middlebury; (800) FOR–PARK or (203) 758–2913; www.quassy.com.

Lemonade Stands across America, page 145: For more information, contact Americares, 88 Hamilton Street, Stamford 06092; (800) 486–HELP.

Cruising, page 146: For information on cruise nights all over the state, contact the Connecticut Council of Car Clubs, P.O. Box 1433, Avon 06001; www.ctccc.org/CruiseNights. For information on Stratford Northeast Cruisers Car Club, contact Ron Passaro at (203) 372–6528.

Photo Credits

Many thanks to the following people and organizations for providing photographs and pictures on the following pages:

© Cecelia M. Barnett for River Rep Theatre Troupe: 49

© Thomas P. Benincas, Jr.: 68 (top left, lower left), 73 (top right), 108, 114, 121 (center right, lower left)

Michael J. Bielawa, *Bridgeport Baseball*

Boundless Playgrounds: 53 (right)

The Bridgeport & Port Jefferson Steamboat Co.: 70

Paula Brisco: 17 (top right), 92 (right), 93, 97

© Les Burdge Photography: 102 (center), 133

Children's Museum of Southeastern Connecticut: 54 (top left)

© Lois E. Clarke for the YMCA of Greater Hartford: 54 (top right)

Connecticut aMAIZEing Maze: 63

Connecticut Opera Association: 36

Connecticut State Library: 71–72

© Dolores Conte: 88 (lower left), 115–16, 132 (top right, lower right)

© ctphotojournalist.com for Boundless Playgrounds: 52, 53 (left)

© Carole Drong: 2–3, 5 (bottom), 18 (top left, center right), 23 (top right, lower left), 29 (top right, lower left), 47 (top left, bottom), 50–51, 57–58, 59 (top left, center right), 82, 96 (center right), 102 (lower left), 105, 121 (lower right), 122–23, 136 (bottom row), 147 (lower right), 148, 156

© Chris Dube: 54 (lower right)

East Woodstock Fourth of July Jamboree: 48 (top right)

The Elm Shakespeare Company: 35

Essex Events Magazine, Essex Printing Co. for Ivoryton Playhouse: 33

Eugene O'Neill Theater Center: 31 (top right, center right)

Sue Evans for Annual Milford Oyster Festival, Inc.: 121 (top right)

Nancy Freeborn: 76 (left), 139

© Susan M. Gilot: 23 (top left, lower right)

The Golden Age of Trucking Museum, Inc.: 60–61

Greater Hartford Arts Council: 26–27

Ron Gustafson for Quassy Amusement Park: 143

Jim Herity for The Maritime Aquarium at Norwalk: 101 (top)

Hillside Equestrian Meadows: 127 (large photo)

Hillard Bloom Shellfish, Inc.: 13

Commander W. V. (Bill) Huling: 117

© Ken Jones for Hot Steamed Jazz Festival: 37 (lower right)

© Frank Kaczmarek: 102 (lower right), 152

Bernadette Kayan, Blue Slope Country Museum & Blue Slope Sawdust, Inc.: 106–07

© Terry Klein: 5 (top), 29 (top left), 47 (top right), 48 (center left, lower right), 59 (top right), 83, 127 (inset)

© 2002 Greg Kriss for Riverfront Recapture: 136 (top right)

Lake Compounce Theme Park: 142

© Steve Laschever for Hartford Symphony Orchestra: 39 (top)

Lime Rock Park: 113 (lower right)

© 1999 Manchester Regional Police and Fire Pipe Band, Inc.: 77–78

The Maritime Aquarium at Norwalk: 100

© Michael Marsland/Yale University: 37 (top right), 150

McCarthy Observatory: 99

© Jack McConnell: 18 (top center), 21 (center right), 29 (lower right), 64, 69 (left), 96 (top right, lower right), 99, 101 (bottom), 104, 110, 111 (bottom), 144 (top)

Peter Morenus/University of Connecticut: 9, 11 (left)

© Lanny Nagler for Hartford Symphony Orchestra: 39 (lower right)

New England Air Museum, Windsor Locks: 79 (right), 80

The New Haven Colony Historical Society: 8

Toshi Otsuki for Victoria Magazine: 55 (left), 56

Cheryl L. Paresi for The Deep River Ancient Muster: 73 (top left)

Jim Paules: 112 (right)

© Charles Perreault, Southington: 119 (top)

Rosemarie Preneta: 55 (right)